AMERICAN POETS PROJECT

AMERICAN POETS PROJECT

IS PUBLISHED WITH A GIFT IN MEMORY OF

James Merrill

AND SUPPORT FROM ITS FOUNDING PATRONS

Sidney J. Weinberg, Jr. Foundation

The Berkley Foundation

Richard B. Fisher and Jeanne Donovan Fisher

American Sonnets

an anthology

david bromwich editor

AMERICAN POETS PROJECT

THE LIBRARY OF AMERICA

The Introduction first appeared, in slightly different form, in *The Yale Review*, April 2005.

Introduction, volume compilation, and notes copyright © 2007 by Literary Classics of the United States, Inc. All rights reserved. Printed in the United States of America. No part of this book may be reproduced in any manner whatsoever without permission.

Some of the material in this volume is reprinted with permission of the holders of copyright and publication rights. Sources and acknowledgments are listed on pages 175–82 and constitute an extension of this copyright page.

The paper used in this publication meets the minimum requirements of the American National Standard for Information Sciences—Permanence of Paper for Printed Library Materials, ANSI Z39.48—1984.

Design by Chip Kidd and Mark Melnick.

Library of Congress Control Number: 2007929878
ISBN 978-1-59853-015-5
American Poets Project—25

10 9 8 7 6 5 4 3 2 1

CONTENTS

INTRODUCTION

American poetry as it first took shape, in the poems of Edward Taylor and Anne Bradstreet, was mainly devotional in character; and though it shifted in the eighteenth century to the satirical mode, and in the nineteenth to a secular subject matter, it did not quickly free itself of English models or find a music of its own. Yet American poets from the first had an unearned bounty, a trove of fresh materials—a gift so omnipresent that we sometimes forget to think of it. Here, in the landscape, were strange memorials of "the mound-builders vanished from the earth," as Bryant recalled in "The Prairies"; in the sky were the big clouds and dragging mists that enchanted Thoreau—"Dew-cloth, dream drapery, / And napkin spread by fays; / Drifting meadow of the air." Here, too, were the familiar appearances Winfield Townley Scott thought Americans should make more of; for "It is so much easier to forget than to have been Mr. Whittier,"

> To stand suddenly struck with wonder of old legends
>   in a young land,
> To look up at last and see poetry driving a buckboard
>   around the bend,

> And poetry all the time in the jays screeching at the
> cats in the dooryard.

The opportunities were here, as Scott reminds us, but it took two hundred years of American living for the poets to stand up and notice. By then, Emerson had prophesied a task for poetry beyond description and chronicle.

His essay "The Poet" freely scatters obiter dicta and imperatives that look far ahead to modernist practice. In this essay you may read, for example, that "The man is only half himself, the other half is his expression"; that "It is not meters, but a meter-making argument that makes a poem"; that "poems are a corrupt version of some text in nature, with which they ought to be made to tally"; that when a poet recovers the truths of nature through imagination, "the meaner the type by which a law is expressed, the more pungent it is, and the more lasting in the memories of men." When poets have realized all this, they will have begun to deserve the vocation Emerson bestows on them: "Poets are thus liberating gods." Emerson spoke his belief again, in a manner just as oracular, in the didactic poem "Merlin," whose hero is instructed not to please by the harmonies of the "trivial harp" but rather to "smite the chords rudely and hard, / As with hammer or with mace," and "mount to paradise / By the stairway of surprise." This imperative—with its suggestion that meters ought to be bracing, irregular, impassioned—would be fulfilled by Whitman in "Song of Myself."

But where does that leave the sonnet? If Emerson were altogether right, there could not be enough American sonnets to make a selection like this. He was, I think, half right. Invention has been prized by American poets above all other qualities; but to the poet of original genius, form is an irrepressible motive to invention. The sonnet is indeed the most settled and traditional of forms. Yet there have been so many good and memorable sonnets by Americans that F. O. Matthiessen, the editor of the great *Oxford Book of American Verse* (1950), confessed one of his leading principles in choosing poems for that anthology had been "not too many sonnets." When Americans turn to this form, they invest it with a glamour and an intensity equal to anything they have to show in more flamboyant or new-minted frames. Relish of the challenge of sonnet-writing, however, seems to have been delayed to the middle of the nineteenth century, and at the turn of the century it was not yet clear how much ground had been won. You may judge how little the change was expected by looking at a sonnet written in despair of sonnets:

> Oh for a poet—for a beacon bright
> To rift this changeless glimmer of dead gray;
> To spirit back the Muses, long astray,
> And flush Parnassus with a newer light;
> To put these little sonnet-men to flight
> Who fashion, in a shrewd mechanic way,
> Songs without souls, that flicker for a day,
> To vanish in irrevocable night.
>
> What does it mean, this barren age of ours?
> Here are the men, the women, and the flowers,
> The seasons, and the sunset, as before.
> What does it mean? Shall there not one arise
> To wrench one banner from the western skies,
> And mark it with his name forevermore?

The gesture that Edwin Arlington Robinson embodies in this poem—his call upon an ancient power to assert the truth of genius in a new setting—is part of the established domain of the sonnet itself. Robinson here does what Wordsworth did when he exclaimed, in one of his *Sonnets on Liberty*, "Milton! thou should'st be living at this hour."

This appeal to a brave predecessor makes an inviolable protest against dead forms—against "the tradition of a fact, the convention of a moral, the straw of last year's harvest," as Browning said in his essay on Shelley. The penultimate line of Robinson's sonnet shows how deeply the aspiration is linked to the motive of his major work: those "western skies" become a signature in poems like "The Dark Hills" and "Luke Havergal" and "The Man Against the Sky." Yet his sonnet against the sonnet-men is not just invective. It is a poem, and it sings, without the seduction of conscious felicity. It sings, even if Robinson's only adjustment of the form to his purpose occurs in the scheme of the sestet: the last rhyme is deferred as a beauty wrung from the drabness of custom. By the end we recognize that this poem is no more a complaint against the sonnet as such than it is a complaint against the sunset. We need the eyes of art to look at society and nature unfettered by habit; that is the power that Robinson would summon again. Poetry in this sense does not tell us how to live, it tells what our living has been while we were looking away. "Here are the men, the women, and the flowers"—just to admit that they are seems a better start for poetry than the "changeless glimmer of dead gray" that comes from imitating other people's imaginative furnishings. The interest of this poem is now in part historical, since Robinson himself performed what he promised: he looked at the men, the women, and the flowers, in major poems that happen to be sonnets, such as "George Crabbe," and pledged to consecrate the "hard, human pulse" that is "throbbing still" in the lives of the lonely and obscure.

The American whose name is most identified with the sonnet is Robert Frost. His predecessors, Wordsworth and Keats, Rossetti and Hopkins, found in the form a characteristic music, but Frost is the author of the best sonnets in

English written by anyone who was not Shakespeare. We can never say why; let us try to see how. In tone and theme, "The Silken Tent" has something in common with "Shall I compare thee to a summer's day?" But there is a difference in its singleness of gesture, an attentiveness that flows into every line and that refuses division into couplet or stanza.

> She is as in a field a silken tent
> At midday when a sunny summer breeze
> Has dried the dew and all its ropes relent,
> So that in guys it gently sways at ease,
> And its supporting central cedar pole,
> That is its pinnacle to heavenward
> And signifies the sureness of the soul,
> Seems to owe naught to any single cord,
> But strictly held by none, is loosely bound
> By countless silken ties of love and thought
> To everything on earth the compass round,
> And only by one's going slightly taut
> In the capriciousness of summer air
> Is of the slightest bondage made aware.

He does it all in a sentence, and this is essential to the figure the poem makes. A well-pitched tent, like a beautiful and poised body, holds its definition whatever the stimuli that press in and distort. Frost works a lovely change here on a celebrated image of sensuous responsiveness from Donne's poem for Elizabeth Drury—"her pure, and eloquent blood, / Spoke in her cheeks, and so distinctly wrought, / That one might almost say, her body thought." Singleness of balance argues singleness of mind—loosely bound, and going taut at the point where sinew or tendon will hold it steady. As a tent moves without pressure when the sun has dried its ropes, so the woman of this poem moves when awakened by some comparable element.

What would that be? Maybe the warmth of the poet himself; or maybe the elements of a day—a tremor caused by a light wind, or something someone said.

What a number of words in this sonnet unerringly prove their rightness for both parts of the metaphor. Let us look at three: "sureness," "capriciousness," and "cord"— the last for a rope but also (by a short stretch for the eye and none for the ear) a chord in music that creates a harmony by which different strains are blended. I have mentioned Donne, but a nearer inspiration of Frost's central idea is a passage in an early poem by Keats, "I stood Tip-toe." When, in Keats's vision of antique beauty, men and maidens have returned from sickness to each other's adoring eyes, nothing needs to be said:

> But the soft numbers, in that moment spoken,
> Made silken ties, that never may be broken.

Frost's declaration of faith comes close to an idea vivid elsewhere in Keats: that the senses teach us to value sensation first in itself, and only later as evidence of something beyond itself. "The Silken Tent" is the sonnet of a lover, caught in a moment of physical admiration, a feeling that goes out from and comes back to the physical body. We know the passion of this poem the more for its suppression of the first-person singular.

"The Silken Tent" speaks of a love of life for its own sake. Turn now to a sonnet about death; or rather about that death-in-life which the most severe and thoughtful New England saints brooded on in their diaries and sermons. Jones Very composed his sonnet "The Dead," just as Frost wrote "The Silken Tent," around a metaphor compressed to a sentence.

> I see them crowd on crowd they walk the earth
> Dry, leafless trees no Autumn wind laid bare;

And in their nakedness find cause for mirth,
And all unclad would winter's rudeness dare;
No sap doth through their clattering branches flow,
Whence springing leaves and blossoms bright
                appear;
Their hearts the living God have ceased to know,
Who gives the spring time to th'expectant year;
They mimic life, as if from him to steal
His glow of health to paint the livid cheek;
They borrow words for thoughts they cannot feel,
That with a seeming heart their tongue may speak;
And in their show of life more dead they live
Than those that to the earth with many tears they
                give.

The final couplet has the sharpness and the stringency
of utter belief. In the case of Very, a disciple of Emerson's
who turned from Unitarianism to a severer faith, the belief
arose from a contrast between the false face and hypocrisy
of those who aim to please God by works, and the grace of
those to whom divine election comes unbidden. We are to
imagine the saved, in this poem, by the unforgiving por-
trait that Very offers of their opposite. His aesthetic criti-
cism has the force of a moral condemnation, and we have
seen this happen before: Robinson's little men "who fash-
ion, in a shrewd mechanic way, / Songs without souls" are
really no different from Very's sapless souls with "clattering
branches," who "borrow words for thoughts they cannot
feel." The power of this harsh poem belongs as much per-
haps to eloquence as to poetry; it has much of the early
New England spirit, unconciliatory and incapable of
wheedling. Very's figures and his phrasing come straight
from the Bible: "Woe unto you, scribes and Pharisees, hyp-
ocrites! for ye are like unto whited sepulchres, which in-
deed appear beautiful outward, but are within full of dead

men's bones, and of all uncleanness." Echoes of Matthew 23:27 and many other verses are woven into the sonnet and refined until they signify an inward discipline.

Jones Very was the tutor at Harvard of another remarkable poet, Frederick Goddard Tuckerman, who lived near Amherst all his life and wrote five sonnet sequences between 1854 and 1872. Tuckerman, as the dates may suggest, was an exact contemporary of Emily Dickinson, and his poems like hers are expressive of intense solitude—a solitude that was chosen not irritably, not therapeutically, but forever and in principle. Dickinson's sense of isolation could be heightened or, to use her own word, *exhilarated* to pitch of ecstasy. No poet or saint has been surer or had less need of confirmation that she was one of the elect. By contrast, Tuckerman's poems are the testament of a lonely man whose loneliness is accepted as a condition of life. In all his work, we are conscious of the recessive instincts of a poet who lives in memory; yet the natural world, of which he is a born observer, makes a constant counterpoint to his reverie. Also, there are moments or glimpses of the society he has cared for: the house for example where two beautiful sisters lived, to whom he devoted a separable group of sonnets. This is the house whose windowpanes, an emblem of memory, he can now hear falling "part by part" into the grassy stones below. Few writers before Tuckerman qualify as poets of nature in the pure and unabstracted manner he sometimes exemplifies. John Clare wrote this way in his shorter lyrics and in verse-rambles where he marked the sights and sounds with a phrase for each; two generations earlier, in the late eighteenth century, William Lisle Bowles had used the sonnet as a variable frame for sheer description; and Tuckerman has something of their assurance, accuracy, and aesthetic continence.

Yet there remains a reserve in his poetry, as Nathaniel Hawthorne commented, a poignancy hidden by the subject matter, a weight of strong emotion always shy of saying more than it means.

> Thin little leaves of wood fern, ribbed and toothed,
> Long curved sail needles of the green pitch pine,
> With common sandgrass, skirt the horizon line,
> And over these the incorruptible blue!
> Here let me gently lie and softly view
> All world asperities, lightly touched and smoothed
> As by his gracious hand, the great Bestower.
> What though the year be late? some colors run
> Yet through the dry, some links of melody.
> Still let me be, by such, assuaged and soothed
> And happier made, as when, our schoolday done,
> We hunted on from flower to frosty flower,
> Tattered and dim, the last red butterfly,
> Or the old grasshopper molasses-mouthed.

You see him lying down, stretched on the grass, and touched to observation by a certain composure of the landscape. The octave and sestet here are nicely interwoven by the rhyme of a natural thing with a metaphysical entity, "flower" and "Bestower": the unremarkable ease of the pair suits the decorum. But those "links of melody" are what anyone will remember this poem for—a synaesthetic metaphor for the red and yellow and brown of the trees in autumn, against the background of gray and dark green. Notice, too, the marvelous closing image that likewise draws upon more than one of the senses, the clicking from stem to stem of the old grasshopper, "molasses-mouthed." Autumn, as we know from his other poems, was Tuckerman's favorite season, and the mixture of elegy is almost conventional in such a mood and setting, but in this sonnet every touch has been felt before being rendered. He wrote two-dozen sonnets as sharply realized as this, somber pictures of an integral life, always within vantage of "the incorruptible blue." He is, as he says of himself elsewhere, one of those who have "gleaned up gold" amid sorrows— "Gold grit and grail, washed from the sands of time."

What accounts for the difference between the major poets who never strike their major note in sonnets— including those, like Dickinson, who by design ignore the form altogether—and poets such as Very and Tuckerman who now seem writers of the first rank largely because of their sonnets? It is a matter of elective affinity with a tradition that either catches or fails to take. One comes to feel that the personality of their perceptions, in these two nineteenth-century masters, was ingrained in their devotion to the sonnet. To them, the form was a second nature. They took up its challenge not as a riddle or a burden, but as a continuous incitement, a welcome test of judgment and passion; so that, word for word and rhyme for rhyme, the sonnet offers the expedient shape in which they most truly come to know themselves. But in the details of their practice, Very and Tuckerman could hardly be more distinct. Very's pattern is the sermon or commentary on a wisdom-text: he seems to have begun all his sonnets from the top, and to have composed by the phrase. By contrast, there never was a poet with a more inborn tact for the "build" toward endings than Tuckerman. Unlike Very, he is not quite at home in his Puritanism or Transcendentalism, but affords a glimpse of something like the elegiac gravity of the Victorians. Though his objects are less fixed and his demeanor far less social, his sonnets of mourning and meditation written over two decades form an impressive American counterpart to Tennyson's *In Memoriam*.

In the twentieth century, after Robinson and Frost,

Edna St. Vincent Millay was the lyric poet who strove for and achieved a mastery of the sonnet with unmistakable freshness and wit. She adapts the form to an urbanity of daily speech that now has commerce with the deeper or glancing encounters of friendship and of love. Her style, though so naturally dramatic, is able to convey an impression of unforced candor in acts of apology or reproof, in seduction as in dismissal, in the blurted regret, the casual confidence, the proud taking of a stand on who and what she is. Her poems belong to the history of an art; and they belong exuberantly to the American 1920s—in this respect showing a clear kinship to the songs of Cole Porter, George and Ira Gershwin, Richard Rodgers and Lorenz Hart. A sonnet like "I shall forget you presently, my dear" has the sort of panache, an elation of spirits after a farewell, that one rightly associates with a song like "You Took Advantage of Me." Millay's early sonnets are a form of speech that carries under it an almost-audible melody. Another aspect of her temperament shows in the sonnets of *Fatal Interview*, one of the few full-length sequences of the modern period that succeed almost throughout. Here, as in the earlier sonnets, Millay chose Shakespeare as an exemplar in the study of erotic pursuit and attachment. She emulated that model as closely as any poet ever has without being overwhelmed.

Both the freedom of Millay's example and the discipline of her work opened a new range of aesthetic experience for younger writers. There were two sexes now in American poetry as in American life. Léonie Adams's "Alas, Kind Element!" is an original sonnet about spring, which finds an erotic undercurrent in the word "alas."

Then I was sealed, and like the wintering tree
I stood me locked upon a summer core;

Living, had died a death, and asked no more.
And I lived then, but as enduringly,
And my heart beat, but only as to be.
Ill weathers well, hail, gust and cold I bore,
I held my life as hid, at root, in store:
Thus I lived then, till this air breathed on me.
Till this kind air breathed kindness everywhere,
There where my times had left me I would stay.
Then I was staunch, I knew nor yes nor no;
But now the wishful leaves have thronged the air.
My every leaf leans forth upon the day;
Alas, kind element! which comes to go.

This sonnet has an idiom that feels archaic because it presses modern words to the limit of their available sense. Adams writes about love as physically as Frost did in "The Silken Tent," but she has a second subject, imagination, and the poem is precise in its capture of a compound feeling: the trap of self-sufficiency, and the regret that comes with its surrender. The words "seal," "locked," "core," and "staunch," are perfectly chosen and placed, as is the repetition of "then" beside its neighbor "there." The first several times I read this poem, it seemed to me that the end required a clinching couplet that had gone missing: it was hard to be offered the long sound of the final word, "go," without an immediate rhyme to match. I no longer think this a weakness. The sense of the words is that the moment of rebirth stole away unheralded, just as it came. It is natural for the poem to end that way as well.

The things we love earliest in the arts are often the things we love best. Tasteful readers may try to forget E. E. Cummings, but there is no escaping him. Sentimentality and sarcasm, panegyric and parody jostle so closely in his poetry that sometimes only a title, a limping or short-footed line, a curl of the lip or a turn of phrase will let you know for sure that a given poem is not offered piously but in ridicule or self-mockery. One good and typical love-and-sex sonnet by Cummings—the one that begins "if I have made,my lady,intricate"—signals its irony only with a space before the drop-down closing line:

> lady through whose profound and fragile lips
> the sweet small clumsy feet of April came
>
> into the ragged meadow of my soul.

Most readers are aware that while Cummings was writing his anti-Petrarchan sonnets—high-spirited attacks on the courtly tradition just as Shakespeare attacked it in "My mistress' eyes are nothing like the sun"—he was also writing sonnets innocent of irony that offer the usual rapturous homage to a gracious lady. What is less well known is that before he wrote the iconoclastic satires and causeries on which his fame chiefly rests, Cummings had written hand-on-heart patriotic hymns in chiming impeccable stanzas, poems of the sort perpetually in demand for use on American children. He wrote them when he was a child himself, and there is no point in quoting. It seems that a firsthand immersion in bombast, suitable for scouting the terrain, went further in his case and left the poet thoroughly soaked in balderdash. No smaller exposure could have produced the undivided gusto of this travesty:

> "next to of course god america i
>   love you land of the pilgrims' and so forth oh
>   say can you see by the dawn's early my
>   country 'tis of centuries come and go
>   and are no more what of it we should worry
>   in every language even deafanddumb
>   thy sons acclaim your glorious name by gorry
>   by jingo by gee by gosh by gum

why talk of beauty what could be more beaut-
iful than these heroic happy dead
who rushed like lions to the roaring slaughter
they did not stop to think they died instead
then shall the voice of liberty be mute?"

He spoke.   And drank rapidly a glass of water

When Dr. Johnson said that patriotism was the last refuge of a scoundrel, he did not mean that patriots tend to be scoundrels, but rather that a scoundrel will always use patriotism as a convenient mask when his other disguises have grown penetrable. The specialty of the patriot-scoundrel, in his militant phase, is a morale that turns public-mindedness into a running faucet of the emotions: hot for chauvinist fervor, cold for bigoted contempt. This poem moves with a cunning alternation of tones between logical-rhetorical ballast ("of course," "what of it?"), re-membered snatches of songs and slogans ("oh say can you see by the dawn's early"), and a broth of random phraseol-ogy ladled up from the timeless clichés of commemoration ("these heroic happy dead / who rushed like lions to the roaring slaughter"). The method employed here, of dip-ping into a private consciousness that turns out to harbor nothing but general-consumption platitudes, may owe something to *Ulysses*—a year or two in print when Cum-mings wrote this sonnet. The same technique would be claimed by John Dos Passos in *U.S.A.*, and by Hart Crane in the opening lines of "The River," where an unamalga-mating medley of voices are overheard, each taking its cue from the last. Crane will make us hear those words as if on the radio, drifting from station to station, but in Cum-mings's poem the channels are in the speaker's head, com-peting, clashing, and most shamelessly harmonizing. The speaker's temperature has gone up considerably by the end. Hence the glass of water. This is a parody no doubt, and its motive is satirical; but does it not, like so much parody and satire, partly love the thing it hates? Cummings's redneck Rotarian blunderbuss of an orator is good enough to make America worth taking a picture of.

Let us look at an experimental sonnet of a slightly later period, "Father" by John Brooks Wheelwright. This poem belongs to a sequence, *Mirrors of Venus*, about friendship and familial piety, and about loyalty and faith. The poet's father is the departed friend to whom he now would turn for conversation and company.

An East Wind asperges Boston with Lynn's
    sulphurous brine.   1
Under the bridge of turrets my father built,—
    from turning sign   1
of CHEVROLET, out-topping our gilt State House
    dome   2
to burning sign of CARTER'S INK,—drip
    multitudes   3
of checker-board shadows. Inverted turreted
    reflections   4
sleeting over axle-grease billows, through all
    directions   4
cross-cut parliamentary gulls, who toss like
    gourds.   3

Speak. Speak to me again, as fresh saddle
    leather   5
(speak; talk again) to a hunter smells of
    heather.   5
Come home. Wire a wire of warning without
    words.   3
Come home and talk to me again, my first
    friend. Father,   5
come home, dead man, who made your mind
    my home.   2

The poem is haunted by a duty to mourn, and an impulse to call his father back to life. At least, that is what I hear in the phrase "Wire a wire of warning": a ghostly Why oh why.

Regret and desolation are the tenor of the poem, but mingled with these is a sense of gratitude and something like hope. The poet's father *has* spoken to him, and will speak again. The city was his city. His spirit now inhabits the crowd of shadows beneath the billboard and neon signs. If this chaos has become the poet's home, his task is to make it more truly a home, through words. Accordingly, "Father" will be the word most rhymed-with, but only at the end, with its sudden vehemence of feeling: these are slant rhymes rather than true, "father," "leather," "heather"—as if to confess that he lent a borrowed potency to things and people that beside him now appear dim and approximate. The rhyme of "dome" with "home," cunningly delayed, underscores the parallel between civic and domestic morale. But the poem has one economy hard to gauge: it lacks two lines, stopping at seven in the pseudo-octave and five in the sestet. Wheelwright, a modernist as instinctive as Joyce, explains the trick in a footnote: "The alexandrine meter makes up a total measure of seventy-two feet though this sonnet lacks two verses of the conventional quota. The second rhyme is far split to keep the ear expectant for the false rhyme on 3." (Look into the numbers and you will see what he means. You get your money's worth of syllables.) As for inward symmetry, we are led early to expect a proper match, a second couplet after the first, to underwrite the portrait of an unfallen city. We are given instead the vague and unsettling "multitudes," with the portrait dissolving in the lines that follow, until his father is called once more to redeem the city and restore the rhyme.

My next example comes from a recent and familiar poet, Elizabeth Bishop. This sonnet is a late poem, one of the last Bishop completed, and it is called, simply, "Sonnet." Yet on the page, it does not look much like a sonnet; it seems a shape-poem, on the order of George Herbert's "Easter Wings." It has an appearance of continuous motion within boundaries, as of liquid passing through a funnel, or jetting from a chasm or fountain.

> Caught—the bubble
> in the spirit-level,
> a creature divided;
> and the compass needle
> wobbling and wavering,
> undecided.
> Freed—the broken
> thermometer's mercury
> running away;
> and the rainbow-bird
> from the narrow bevel
> of the empty mirror,
> flying wherever
> it feels like, gay!

The poem is an allegory built from a few oppositions: confinement, freedom; division, unity; uncertainty, purpose; imitation, originality; life, immortality. A covenant has been made with the soul, and what it promised is performed in the startling release of the last lines. All the implications are joined in the elusive and philosophical word "gay," to denote a happiness within, a joy at last unencumbered by fortune or circumstance.

In structure, Bishop's is a reverse sonnet, six lines in the first half, eight in the second, with three true rhymes: *divided/undecided* and *level/bevel* connect the halves of the poem from afar; *away/gay* links the ninth line and the fourteenth, and allows the ear to read the poem as an eight-six sonnet after all. The tightness seems an effect created by something more than Bishop's careful work with a few metaphors, though that is certainly all-important for the rhythm of containment and release: the spirit-level (a carpenter's tool, here with a metaphysical sense), the compass needle, and the thermometer mercury. They are three of a kind—but what to make of the "rainbow-bird" flying out of the empty mirror? A ghost is the only thing in the world that leaves no reflection in a mirror, and in the same family of words as "ghost" you will find "aghast" (the other side of gay) and "*Geist*" (spirit). Bishop is writing of the surprise to the soul imparted by the vision, or by the experience, of freedom. This sonnet is the record of a discovery of joy. It could not be even a syllable longer and be so purely what it is.

All the sonnets I have discussed so far have been observant and expressive in a high degree; but with the exception of Cummings's, their dominant mood is a kind of self-regard. The poet is thinking for himself or herself. Indeed, our sense of their integrity comes from the conveyed effect of a solitary experience. Now there is a time-honored objection to modern poetry, which goes back to Keats's strictures on what he called "the egotistical sublime." Yes, you are sublime (Keats said to Wordsworth and to modern poets generally), but look at the cost to your powers of sympathy. A fair response might be to concede the point and turn the tables on the questioner. Are the rewards really so slender? But this may admit the truth of the charge too readily. There are modern poems by Hardy and Yeats and Frost, among others, that are not just exceptions to the rule but exceptions so vast they seem to call for a different description. I close with another sonnet by Frost, which may make the work of description unnecessary.

"The Master Speed" is a poem about love that is

strong without hyperbole. It has a second subject, friendship, considered not as the precursor but as the accompaniment of love. Yet these larger relations are tracked on the way to its being a poem in praise of marriage; or rather, an encouragement offered to a particular couple, Irma Frost and John Cone, on October 15, 1926. Frost liked the man his daughter was going to marry; we feel this without its having to be said. So it is very much an occasional poem, written to be spoken at the wedding, and, as with other such poems, we may wish to extend its hope to ourselves; but that feeling does not diminish our interest in the man and woman who inspired this public act of private speech.

> No speed of wind or water rushing by
> But you have speed far greater. You can climb
> Back up a stream of radiance to the sky,
> And back through history up the stream of time.
> And you were given this swiftness, not for haste
> Nor chiefly that you may go where you will,
> But in the rush of everything to waste,
> That you may have the power of standing still—
> Off any still or moving thing you say.
> Two such as you with such a master speed
> Cannot be parted nor be swept away
> From one another once you are agreed
> That life is only life forevermore
> Together wing to wing and oar to oar.

Frost's "you" seems to salute any of us. It is said in a broad yet also an intimate tone, a blend that few poets have controlled so capably. But the real "you" whom the poem means to address are the pair who together make this marriage.

One such as you would be prodigious, but to have found two! (That calls for a sonnet.) Marriage will change what each of them is, without making either less energetic or original: this is the poet's conceit and the consolation he offers. So his final lines at once cement and celebrate an agreement that runs parallel to the marriage vow, "That life is only life forevermore / Together wing to wing and oar to oar." Note that the wonderful closing lines are unpunctuated. They could not bear punctuation. Life is only life—it might stop there: a flat and honorable understatement, such as one hears from the characters in Frost's dramatic poems and dialogues. Life is only life *forevermore* passes on to a solemn and even a religious vow, touched, maybe, by a wish to add a clause to the contract while pretending not to exaggerate. Life is only life forevermore *together*: there you have the wish alongside the matter of fact. This man and wife will work in earnest at any task they resolve to work at. And to assure their progress, the poet equips them with instruments both natural and acquired, growing out of the body and improving on it. Wing to wing and oar to oar.

And yet there remains a doubt that cannot be appeased. This poem about friendship and marriage is haunted by an idea of destruction, "the rush of everything to waste." The desire to slow the rush is a possible and not a selfish motive for having children; and with this in mind, the poem sets beside destruction a curious opposite: the fascination of *choosing*. This may mean above all choosing to stand still; but "the power of standing still" is ambiguous: maintaining a former stance or standing motionless. Emerson included both kinds of standing in the opening paragraph of "Self-Reliance" when he declared that all original actions and works of art "teach us to abide by our spontaneous impression with good-humored inflexibility then most when the whole cry of voices is on the other side." Frost has remembered that advice. Still, it is one thing to say this to a reader, another to speak it as the relevant blessing to a man and a woman starting their life together. How can the poet reckon the consequences for them?

Frost's sonnet brings out the meaning of their pact—it dramatizes their choice, deliberately and delicately—by organizing itself into a sonnet twice over. The formally apt break for the sestet occurs when the two of them stand away from the crowd, and a full dash marks the choice: "— / Off any still or moving thing you say." But then, as it were unofficially, the sestet begins its own resolution five lines from the end, with the phrase "Two such as you." These two, who know in themselves the power of standing still, have joined as one that cannot be parted. The ancestor of Frost's sonnet is Shakespeare's "The Phoenix and Turtle," but that poem's idea of unity-in-division was Christian, whereas Frost, with a radicalism of conviction and craft, returns the paradox to its Platonic source. Man and woman were born one before they were made two. Their union, however, takes on a greater dignity when viewed as a choice than it could possibly have as a thing merely given.

Maverick experiment and enterprise, the frankness and the unconcern of Whitman's "barbaric yawp," these have been qualities fairly enough identified with American poetry. Their presence has never excluded the singular purpose and the compositional economy that belong properly to the sonnet; and the present anthology aims to exhibit the variety of objects that have come under that description. Early in the last century, there was a crisis of belief in conventional forms, which made poets and critics think hard about why a tradition like the sonnet should persist. Responding to this situation in "Reflections on *Vers Libre*" (1917), T. S. Eliot observed that modern poets could renew old genres such as mock-epic even as they burned through more recently favored modes like the naturalist novel. His prognosis was uncertain. "We only need the coming of a satirist," Eliot guessed, "to prove that the heroic couplet has lost none of its edge since Dryden and Pope laid it down," but other forms were in direr straits: "As for the sonnet I am not so sure." Newness was not the determiner of value, for Eliot; of *vers libre* he remarked "it is the battle cry of freedom, and there is no freedom in art." But with his well-earned skepticism, he almost persuaded himself that the sonnet was dead. The pages that follow will show how much evidence already existed for a more appreciative judgment. Yet one must sympathize with Eliot, as with all critics who, canvassing the history of an art, are drawn to speculate reasonably about its future. There was no good reason for the sonnet to be reborn in America, except that the thoughts and feelings of poets turned out to be renewable under this aspect, close as the form is to aria and aphorism, close to syllogism, close to prayer.

David Bromwich
2007

A NOTE ON THE SONNET

The sonnet was perfected by Petrarch, in fourteenth-century Italy; its first subject matter was sexual love. The great English sequences by Sidney, Spenser, and Shakespeare enlarged the Italian tradition by mingling the actual and imaginative experiences of the poet with the idealisms of love. Milton and Donne in the seventeenth century further widened its range to encompass admiration for acts of public virtue and the utterance of prayer in verse. Yet the Renaissance hierarchy and separation of genres had a long afterlife, so that a modern like Yeats in "Leda and the Swan" —a sonnet that mixes the pagan theology, a description of a rape, and the prophecy of an impending catastrophe— could still shock readers whose taste had been partly formed on classical models. Since the Romantic period, however, the sonnet has claimed a unique aesthetic prestige. It is a field of exercise for concentrated virtuosity, an invitation to soar and only touch the ground when speech has magically rounded itself, a pattern so resonant that a poet can scarcely write a poem of fourteen lines without courting the genre or somehow alluding to its past. Displacement or suggestive suppression of rhyme may make as true an *homage* as any overt echo. Whether divided into sections of eight lines and six (octave and sestet), three quatrains and a closing couplet, twelve lines and a couplet, or fourteen at once, the sonnet is a place for intense avowal or meditation, the fixing of a compact and memorable record where the subject is found, held, and framed as if in a single pulse of thought and feeling.

D.B.

JOHN QUINCY ADAMS | 1767–1848

To the Sun-Dial

Under the Window of the Hall
of the House of Representatives of the United States

Thou silent herald of Time's silent flight!
   Say, could'st thou speak, what warning voice
       were thine?
   Shade, who canst only show how others shine!
Dark, sullen witness of resplendent light
In day's broad glare, and when the noontide bright
   Of laughing fortune sheds the ray divine,
   Thy ready favors cheer us—but decline
The clouds of morning and the gloom of night.
Yet are thy counsels faithful, just, and wise;
   They bid us seize the moments as they pass—
Snatch the retrieveless sunbeam as it flies,
   Nor lose one sand of life's revolving glass—
Aspiring still, with energy sublime,
By virtuous deeds to give eternity to Time.

On the Luxembourg Gallery

There is a charm no vulgar mind can reach,
No critic thwart, no mighty master teach;
A charm how mingled of the good and ill!
Yet still so mingled that the mystic whole
Shall captive hold the struggling gazer's will,
Till vanquished reason own its full control.
And such, O Rubens, thy mysterious art,
The charm that vexes, yet enslaves the heart!
Thy lawless style, from timid systems free,
Impetuous rolling like a troubled sea,
High o'er the rocks of reason's lofty verge
Impending hangs; yet, ere the foaming surge
Breaks o'er the bound, the refluent ebb of taste
Back from the shore impels the watery waste.

WILLIAM CULLEN BRYANT | 1794–1878

November

Yet one smile more, departing distant sun!
    One mellow smile through the soft vapory air,
Ere, o'er the frozen earth, the loud winds run,
    Or snows are sifted o'er the meadows bare.
One smile on the brown hills and naked trees,
    And the dark rocks whose summer wreaths are cast,
And the blue Gentian flower, that, in the breeze,
    Nods lonely, of her beauteous race the last.
Yet a few sunny days, in which the bee
    Shall murmur by the hedge that skirts the way,
The cricket chirp upon the russet lea,
    And man delight to linger in thy ray.
Yet one rich smile, and we will try to bear
The piercing winter frost, and winds, and darkened air.

To an American Painter Departing for Europe

Thine eyes shall see the light of distant skies:
    Yet, Cole! thy heart shall bear to Europe's strand
    A living image of thy native land,
Such as on thy own glorious canvass lies.
Lone lakes—savannahs where the bison roves—
    Rocks rich with summer garlands—solemn streams—
    Skies, where the desert eagle wheels and screams—
Spring bloom and autumn blaze of boundless groves.
Fair scenes shall greet thee where thou goest—fair,
    But different—every where the trace of men,
    Paths, homes, graves, ruins, from the lowest glen
To where life shrinks from the fierce Alpine air.
    Gaze on them, till the tears shall dim thy sight,
    But keep that earlier, wilder image bright.

Mezzo Cammin

Half of my life is gone, and I have let
    The years slip from me and have not fulfilled
    The aspiration of my youth, to build
    Some tower of song with lofty parapet.
Not indolence, nor pleasure, nor the fret
    Of restless passions that would not be stilled,
    But sorrow, and a care that almost killed,
    Kept me from what I may accomplish yet;
Though, half-way up the hill, I see the Past
    Lying beneath me with its sounds and sights,—
    A city in the twilight dim and vast,
With smoking roofs, soft bells, and gleaming lights,—
    And hear above me on the autumnal blast
    The cataract of Death far thundering from the
        heights.

FROM **Divina Commedia**

I

Oft have I seen at some cathedral door
    A laborer, pausing in the dust and heat,
    Lay down his burden, and with reverent feet
    Enter, and cross himself, and on the floor
Kneel to repeat his paternoster o'er;
    Far off the noises of the world retreat;
    The loud vociferations of the street
    Become an undistinguishable roar.
So, as I enter here from day to day,
    And leave my burden at this minster gate,
    Kneeling in prayer, and not ashamed to pray,
The tumult of the time disconsolate
    To inarticulate murmurs dies away,
    While the eternal ages watch and wait.

The Sound of the Sea

The sea awoke at midnight from its sleep,
 And round the pebbly beaches far and wide
 I heard the first wave of the rising tide
 Rush onward with uninterrupted sweep;
A voice out of the silence of the deep,
 A sound mysteriously multiplied
 As of a cataract from the mountain's side,
 Or roar of winds upon a wooded steep.
So comes to us at times, from the unknown
 And inaccessible solitudes of being,
 The rushing of the sea-tides of the soul;
And inspirations, that we deem our own,
 Are some divine foreshadowing and foreseeing
 Of things beyond our reason or control.

Nature

As a fond mother, when the day is o'er,
    Leads by the hand her little child to bed,
    Half willing, half reluctant to be led,
    And leave his broken playthings on the floor,
Still gazing at them through the open door,
    Nor wholly reassured and comforted
    By promises of others in their stead,
    Which, though more splendid, may not please him
        more;
So Nature deals with us, and takes away
    Our playthings one by one, and by the hand
    Leads us to rest so gently, that we go
Scarce knowing if we wish to go or stay,
    Being too full of sleep to understand
    How far the unknown transcends the what we know.

The Harvest Moon

It is the Harvest Moon! On gilded vanes
    And roofs of villages, on woodland crests
    And their aerial neighborhoods of nests
    Deserted, on the curtained window-panes
Of rooms where children sleep, on country lanes
    And harvest-fields, its mystic splendor rests!
    Gone are the birds that were our summer guests;
    With the last sheaves return the laboring wains!
All things are symbols: the external shows
    Of Nature have their image in the mind,
    As flowers and fruits and falling of the leaves;
The song-birds leave us at the summer's close,
    Only the empty nests are left behind,
    And pipings of the quail among the sheaves.

The Cross of Snow

In the long, sleepless watches of the night,
    A gentle face—the face of one long dead—
    Looks at me from the wall, where round its head
    The night-lamp casts a halo of pale light.
Here in this room she died; and soul more white
    Never through martyrdom of fire was led
    To its repose; nor can in books be read
    The legend of a life more benedight.
There is a mountain in the distant West
    That, sun-defying, in its deep ravines
    Displays a cross of snow upon its side.
Such is the cross I wear upon my breast
    These eighteen years, through all the changing scenes
    And seasons, changeless since the day she died.

To Science

Science! true daughter of Old Time thou art!
    Who alterest all things with thy peering eyes.
Why preyest thou thus upon the poet's heart,
    Vulture, whose wings are dull realities?
How should he love thee? or how deem thee wise,
    Who wouldst not leave him in his wandering
To seek for treasure in the jewelled skies,
    Albeit he soared with an undaunted wing?
Hast thou not dragged Diana from her car?
    And driven the Hamadryad from the wood
To seek a shelter in some happier star?
    Hast thou not torn the Naiad from her flood,
The Elfin from the green grass, and from me
The summer dream beneath the tamarind tree?

The Columbine

Still, still my eye will gaze long-fixed on thee,
Till I forget that I am called a man,
And at thy side fast-rooted seem to be,
And the breeze comes my cheek with thine to fan;
Upon this craggy hill our life shall pass,
A life of summer days and summer joys,
Nodding our honey bells mid pliant grass
In which the bee half hid his time employs;
And here we'll drink with thirsty pores the rain,
And turn dew-sprinkled to the rising sun,
And look when in the flaming west again
His orb across the heaven its path has run;
Here, left in darkness on the rocky steep,
My weary eyes shall close like folding flowers in sleep.

The New Birth

'Tis a new life—thoughts move not as they did
With slow uncertain steps across my mind,
In thronging haste fast pressing on they bid
The portals open to the viewless wind;
That comes not, save when in the dust is laid
The crown of pride that gilds each mortal brow,
And from before man's vision melting fade
The heavens and earth—Their walls are falling now—
Fast crowding on each thought claims utterance strong,
Storm-lifted waves swift rushing to the shore
On from the sea they send their shouts along,
Back through the cave-worn rocks their thunders roar,
And I a child of God by Christ made free
Start from death's slumbers to eternity.

The Garden

I saw the spot where our first parents dwelt;
And yet it wore to me no face of change,
For while amid its fields and groves I felt
As if I had not sinned, nor thought it strange;
My eye seemed but a part of every sight,
My ear heard music in each sound that rose,
Each sense forever found a new delight,
Such as the spirit's vision only knows;
Each act some new and ever-varying joy
Did by my Father's love for me prepare;
To dress the spot my ever fresh employ,
And in the glorious whole with Him to share;
No more without the flaming gate to stray,
No more for sin's dark stain the debt of death to pay.

The Latter Rain

The latter rain, it falls in anxious haste
Upon the sun-dried fields and branches bare,
Loosening with searching drops the rigid waste
As if it would each root's lost strength repair;
But not a blade grows green as in the spring,
No swelling twig puts forth its thickening leaves;
The robins only mid the harvests sing
Pecking the grain that scatters from the sheaves;
The rain falls still—the fruit all ripened drops,
It pierces chestnut burr and walnut shell,
The furrowed fields disclose the yellow crops,
Each bursting pod of talents used can tell,
And all that once received the early rain
Declare to man it was not sent in vain.

The Dead

I see them crowd on crowd they walk the earth
Dry, leafless trees no Autumn wind laid bare;
And in their nakedness find cause for mirth,
And all unclad would winter's rudeness dare;
No sap doth through their clattering branches flow,
Whence springing leaves and blossoms bright appear;
Their hearts the living God have ceased to know,
Who gives the spring time to th'expectant year;
They mimic life, as if from him to steal
His glow of health to paint the livid cheek;
They borrow words for thoughts they cannot feel,
That with a seeming heart their tongue may speak;
And in their show of life more dead they live
Than those that to the earth with many tears they give.

Thy Brother's Blood

I have no Brother—they who meet me now
Offer a hand with their own wills defiled,
And while they wear a smooth unwrinkled brow
Know not that Truth can never be beguiled;
Go wash the hand that still betrays thy guilt;
Before the spirit's gaze what stain can hide?
Abel's red blood upon the earth is spilt,
And by thy tongue it cannot be denied;
I hear not with the ear—the heart doth tell
Its secret deeds to me untold before;
Go, all its hidden plunder quickly sell,
Then shalt thou cleanse thee from thy brother's gore;
Then will I take thy gift—that bloody stain
Shall not be seen upon thy hand again.

Nature

The bubbling brook doth leap when I come by,
Because my feet find measure with its call;
The birds know when the friend they love is nigh,
For I am known to them both great and small;
The flowers, which on the lovely hill-side grow,
Expect me there, when Spring their bloom has given;
And many a bush and tree my wanderings know,
And e'en the clouds and silent stars of heaven:
For he, who with his Maker walks aright,
Shall be their lord, as Adam was before;
His ear shall catch each sound with new delight,
Each object wear the dress that then it wore;
And he, as when erect in soul he stood,
Hear from his Father's lips that all is good.

The Children

I saw, strange sight! the children sat at meat,
When they their Parent's face had never known;
Nor rose they when they heard his step to greet,
But feasted there upon his gifts alone;
'Twas morn, and noon, and evening hour the same;
They heeded not 'twas He who gave them bread;
For they had not yet learned to call his name,
They had been children, but they now were dead;
Yet still their Father, with a father's care,
Early and late stood waiting by their board;
Hoping each hour that they his love would share,
And at his table sit to life restored;
Alas! for many a day and year I stood
And saw them feasting thus yet knew not Him how good.

Autumn Leaves

The leaves though thick are falling; one by one
Decayed they drop from off their parent tree;
Their work with autumn's latest day is done,
Thou see'st them borne upon its breezes free;
They lie strown here and there, their many dyes
That yesterday so caught thy passing eye;
Soiled by the rain each leaf neglected lies,
Upon the path where now thou hurriest by;
Yet think thee not their beauteous tints less fair,
Than when they hung so gaily o'er thy head;
But rather find thee eyes, and look thee there
Where now thy feet so heedless o'er them tread;
And thou shalt see where wasting now they lie,
The unseen hues of immortality.

The Barberry Bush

The bush which bears most briars, and bitter fruit,
Waits till the frost has turned its green leaves red,
Its sweetened berries will thy palate suit,
And thou may'st find, e'en there, a homely bread.
Upon the hills of Salem, scattered wide,
Their yellow blossoms gain the eye in Spring;
And straggling down upon the turnpike's side,
Their ripened bunches to your hand they bring.
I've plucked them oft in boyhood's early hour,
What then I gave such name, and thought it true;
But now I know, that other fruit, as sour,
Grows on what now thou callest *Me*, and *You*;
Yet, wilt thou wait the Autumn that I see,
'Twill sweeter taste than these red berries be.

The Hand and Foot

The hand and foot that stir not, they shall find
Sooner than all the rightful place to go;
Now in their motion free as roving wind,
Though first no snail so limited and slow;
I mark them full of labor all the day,
Each active motion made in perfect rest;
They cannot from their path mistaken stray,
Though 'tis not theirs, yet in it they are blest;
The bird has not their hidden track found out,
Nor cunning fox though full of art he be;
It is the way unseen, the certain route,
Where ever bound, yet thou art ever free;
The path of Him, whose perfect law of love
Bids spheres and atoms in just order move.

Yourself

'Tis to yourself I speak; you cannot know
Him whom I call in speaking such an one,
For thou beneath the earth liest buried low,
Which he alone as living walks upon;
Thou mayst at times have heard him speak to you,
And often wished perchance that you were he;
And I must ever wish that it were true,
For then thou couldst hold fellowship with me;
But now thou hearst us talk as strangers, met
Above the room wherein thou liest abed;
A word perhaps loud spoken thou mayst get,
Or hear our feet when heavily they tread;
But he who speaks, or him who's spoken to,
Must both remain as strangers still to you.

The Lost

The fairest day that ever yet has shone,
Will be when thou the day within shalt see;
The fairest rose that ever yet has blown,
When thou the flower thou lookest on shalt be.
But thou art far away among Time's toys;
Thyself the day thou lookest for in them,
Thyself the flower that now thine eye enjoys,
But wilted now thou hang'st upon thy stem.
The bird thou hearest on the budding tree,
Thou hast made sing with thy forgotten voice;
But when it swells again to melody,
The song is thine in which thou wilt rejoice;
And thou new risen 'midst these wonders live,
That now to them dost all thy substance give.

FROM **The Origin of Man**

I

Man has forgot his Origin; in vain
He searches for the record of his race
In ancient books, or seeks with toil to gain
From the deep cave, or rocks some primal trace.
And some have fancied, from a higher sphere,
Forgetful of his origin he came;
To dwell awhile a wandering exile here
Subject to sense, another, yet the same.
With mind bewildered, weak how should he know
The Source Divine from whom his being springs?
The darkened spirit does its shadow throw
On written record, and on outward things;
That else might plainly to his thought reveal
The wondrous truths, which now they but conceal.

HENRY DAVID THOREAU | 1817–1862

FROM **A Week on the Concord and Merrimack Rivers**

This is my Carnac, whose unmeasured dome
Shelters the measuring art and measurer's home.
Behold these flowers, let us be up with time,
Not dreaming of three thousand years ago,
Erect ourselves and let those columns lie,
Not stoop to raise a foil against the sky.
Where is the spirit of that time but in
This present day, perchance the present line?
Three thousand years ago are not agone,
They are still lingering in this summer morn,
And Memnon's Mother sprightly greets us now,
Wearing her youthful radiance on her brow.
If Carnac's columns still stand on the plain,
To enjoy our opportunities they remain.

The Street

They pass me by like shadows, crowds on crowds,
Dim ghosts of men, that hover to and fro,
Hugging their bodies round them, like thin shrouds
Wherein their souls were buried long ago:
They trampled on their youth, and faith, and love,
They cast their hope of human-kind away,
With Heaven's clear messages they madly strove,
And conquered,—and their spirits turned to clay:
Lo! how they wander round the world, their grave,
Whose ever-gaping maw by such is fed,
Gibbering at living men, and idly rave,
"We, only, truly live, but ye are dead."
Alas! poor fools, the anointed eye may trace
A dead soul's epitaph in every face!

FREDERICK GODDARD TUCKERMAN | 1821–1873

FROM **Sonnets, First Series**

VII

Dank fens of cedar, hemlock branches gray
With trees and trail of mosses, wringing-wet,
Beds of the black pitchpine in dead leaves set
Whose wasted red has wasted to white away,
Remnants of rain and droppings of decay,
Why hold ye so my heart, nor dimly let
Through your deep leaves the light of yesterday,
The faded glimmer of a sunshine set?
Is it that in your darkness, shut from strife,
The bread of tears becomes the bread of life?
Far from the roar of day, beneath your boughs
Fresh griefs beat tranquilly, and loves and vows
Grow green in your gray shadows, dearer far
Even than all lovely lights and roses are?

X

An upper chamber in a darkened house,
Where, ere his footsteps reached ripe manhood's brink,
Terror and anguish were his lot to drink;
I cannot rid the thought nor hold it close
But dimly dream upon that man alone:
Now though the autumn clouds most softly pass,
The cricket chides beneath the doorstep stone
And greener than the season grows the grass.
Nor can I drop my lids nor shade my brows,
But there he stands beside the lifted sash;
And with a swooning of the heart, I think
Where the black shingles slope to meet the boughs
And, shattered on the roof like smallest snows,
The tiny petals of the mountain ash.

XXVIII

Not the round natural world, not the deep mind,
The reconcilement holds: the blue abyss
Collects it not; our arrows sink amiss
And but in Him may we our import find.
The agony to know, the grief, the bliss
Of toil, is vain and vain: clots of the sod
Gathered in heat and haste and flung behind
To blind ourselves and others, what but this
Still grasping dust and sowing toward the wind?
No more thy meaning seek, thine anguish plead,
But leaving straining thought and stammering word,
Across the barren azure pass to God:
Shooting the void in silence like a bird,
A bird that shuts his wings for better speed.

VII

His heart was in his garden; but his brain
Wandered at will among the fiery stars.
Bards, heroes, prophets, Homers, Hamilcars,
With many angels stood, his eye to gain;
The devils, too, were his familiars:
And yet the cunning florist held his eyes
Close to the ground, a tulip bulb his prize,
And talked of tan and bonedust, cutworms, grubs,
As though all Nature held no higher strain;
Or, if he spoke of art, he made the theme
Flow through boxborders, turf, and flower tubs
Or, like a garden engine's, steered the stream,
Now spouted rainbows to the silent skies,
Now kept it flat and raked the walks and shrubs.

XV

Gertrude and Gulielma, sister-twins,
Dwelt in the valley at the farmhouse old;
Nor grief had touched their locks of dark and gold
Nor dimmed the fragrant whiteness of their skins:
Both beautiful, and one in height and mould;
Yet one had loveliness which the spirit wins
To other worlds: eyes, forehead, smile and all,
More softly serious than the twilight's fall.
The other—can I e'er forget the day
When, stealing from a laughing group away,
To muse with absent eye and motion slow,
Her beauty fell upon me like a blow?—
Gertrude! with red flowerlip, and silk black hair!
Yet Gulielma was by far more fair.

XVI

Under the mountain, as when first I knew
Its low dark roof and chimney creeper-twined,
The red house stands; and yet my footsteps find,
Vague in the walks, waste balm and feverfew.
But they are gone: no soft-eyed sisters trip
Across the porch or lintels; where, behind,
The mother sat, sat knitting with pursed lip.
The house stands vacant in its green recess,
Absent of beauty as a broken heart.
The wild rain enters, and the sunset wind
Sighs in the chambers of their loveliness
Or shakes the pane—and in the silent noons
The glass falls from the window, part by part,
And ringeth faintly in the grassy stones.

XVIII

And change with hurried hand has swept these scenes:
The woods have fallen, across the meadow-lot
The hunter's trail and trap-path is forgot,
And fire has drunk the swamps of evergreens;
Yet for a moment let my fancy plant
These autumn hills again: the wild dove's haunt,
The wild deer's walk. In golden umbrage shut,
The Indian river runs, Quonecktacut!
Here, but a lifetime back, where falls tonight
Behind the curtained pane a sheltered light
On buds of rose or vase of violet
Aloft upon the marble mantel set,
Here in the forest-heart, hung blackening
The wolfbait on the bush beside the spring.

XXIX

How oft in schoolboy-days, from the school's sway
Have I run forth to Nature as to a friend,
With some pretext of o'erwrought sight, to spend
My schooltime in green meadows far away!
Careless of summoning bell or clocks that strike,
I marked with flowers the minutes of my day.
For still the eye that shrank from hated hours,
Dazzled with decimal and dividend,
Knew each bleached alder root that plashed across
The bubbling brook, and every mass of moss;
Could tell the month, too, by the vervain-spike,
How far the ring of purple tiny flowers
Had climbed—just starting, maybe, with the May,
Half-high, or tapering off at summer's end.

XXX

Yet even mid merry boyhood's tricks and scapes,
Early my heart a deeper lesson learnt:
Wandering alone by many a mile of burnt
Black woodside, that but the snowflake decks and
    drapes;
And I have stood beneath Canadian sky
In utter solitudes, where the cricket's cry
Appals the heart, and fear takes visible shapes;
And on Long Island's void and isolate capes
Heard the sea break like iron bars. And still
In all I seemed to hear the same deep dirge
Borne in the wind, the insect's tiny trill,
And crash and jangle of the shaking surge,
And knew not what they meant, prophetic woe?
Dim bodings wherefore? Now indeed I know.

XXXII

O for the face and footstep! woods and shores
That looked upon us in life's happiest flush,
That saw our figures breaking from the brush;
That heard our voices calling through the bowers,
How are ye darkened! Deepest tears upgush
From the heart's heart, gathering more and more
Blindness and strangling tears, as now before
Your shades I stand and find ye still so fair.
And thou, sad mountain stream, thy stretches steal
Through fern and flag as when we gathered flowers
Along thy reeds and shallows cold, or where—
Over the red reef with a rolling roar—
The woods through glimmering gaps of green reveal,
Sideward, the river turning like a wheel.

IV

Thin little leaves of wood fern, ribbed and toothed,
Long curved sail needles of the green pitch pine,
With common sandgrass, skirt the horizon line,
And over these the incorruptible blue!
Here let me gently lie and softly view
All world asperities, lightly touched and smoothed
As by his gracious hand, the great Bestower.
What though the year be late? some colors run
Yet through the dry, some links of melody.
Still let me be, by such, assuaged and soothed
And happier made, as when, our schoolday done,
We hunted on from flower to frosty flower,
Tattered and dim, the last red butterfly,
Or the old grasshopper molasses-mouthed.

VI

I looked across the rollers of the deep,
Long land-swells, ropes of weed, and riding foam,
With bitter angry heart: did I not roam
Ever like these? And what availeth sleep?
Or wakefulness? or pain? And still the sea
Rustled and sang, "Alike! and one to me!"
Ay! once I trod these shores too happily,
Murmuring my gladness to the rocks and ground
And, while the wave broke loud on ledge and reef,
Whispered it in the pause, like one who tells
His heart's dream and delight! And still the sea
Went back and forth upon its bar of shells,
Washed and withdrew, with a soft shaling sound,
As though the wet were dry and joy were grief.

VII

O rest divine! O golden certainty
Of love! when love's half smile, illumining pain,
Bade all bright things immutable remain.
Dreaming I stand, the low brook drawling by,
Her flowerlike mien, her mountain step to mark.
Ah, I recall when her least look again
Could mar the music in my happy mind
And plunge me into doubt, her faintest sigh
Stir all the fixed pillars of my heaven,
Commingling them in mist and stormy dark!
And all together, as I have seen the rain
When the whole shower is swinging in the wind,
And like a mighty pendulum urged and driven,
Beat back and forth between the earth and sky!

IX

But into order falls our life at last,
Though in the retrospection jarred and blent.
Broken ambition, love misplaced or spent
Too soon, and slander busy with the past:
Sorrows too sweet to lose, or vexing joy.
But Time will bring oblivion of annoy,
And Silence bind the blows that words have lent;
And we will dwell, unheeding Love or Fame
Like him who has outlived a shining Name:
And Peace will come, as evening comes to him,
No leader now of men, no longer proud
But poor and private, watching the sun's rim;
Contented too, to fade as yonder cloud
Dim fades, and as the sun fades, fades alike, like dim.

X

Sometimes I walk where the deep water dips
Against the land. Or on where fancy drives
I walk and muse aloud, like one who strives
To tell his half-shaped thought with stumbling lips,
And view the ocean sea, the ocean ships,
With joyless heart: still but myself I find
And restless phantoms of my restless mind:
Only the moaning of my wandering words,
Only the wailing of the wheeling plover,
And this high rock beneath whose base the sea
Has wormed long caverns, like my tears in me:
And hard like this I stand, and beaten and blind,
This desolate rock with lichens rusted over,
Hoar with salt-sleet and chalkings of the birds.

I

Still, like a city, seated on a height
Appears my soul, and gathered in her place:
Whilst, faintly hovering, swarm about her base,
Still nearer drawing with the nearer night,
Dim cloudlike groups of men and groups of horse,
Outposts and riders of some mightier Force
That lies along the hills; while from them thrown
Rise shadowing shafts with storms of summoning stone,
And the bolt falleth where the cross-bolt fell;
Till Doubt contends with Hope, and Fear conspires
To thwart them both: so that the soul retires
Even to her inmost keep and citadel
And views along the horizon darkening far,
Vague tumult, lights of woe, and moving war.

VIII

Nor strange it is, to us who walk in bonds
Of flesh and time, if virtue's self awhile
Gleam dull like sunless ice; whilst graceful guile—
Blood-flecked like hamatite or diamonds
With a red inward spark—to reconcile
Beauty and evil seems and corresponds
So well with good that the mind joys to have
Full wider jet and scope: nor swings and sleeps
Forever in one cradle wearily
Like those vast weeds that off d'Acunha's isle
Wash with the surf and flap their mighty fronds
Mournfully to the dipping of the wave,
Yet cannot be disrupted from their deeps
By the whole heave and settle of the sea.

III

And yet tonight, when summer daylight dies,
I crossed the fields against the summer gust
And with me, rising from my feet like dust,
A crowd of flea-like grasshoppers, like flies
Presaging dry and dry continuance; yet
Where they prefigure change, all signals must
Fail in the dry when they forbode the wet . . .
I know not. All tonight seemed mystery:
From the full fields that pressed so heavily,
The burden of the blade, the waste of blowth,
The twinkling of the smallest life that flits
To where, and all unconsciously, he sits:
My little boy, symbolling eternity,
Like the god Brahma, with his toe in his mouth.

XVI

Let me give something!—as the years unfold,
Some faint fruition, though not much, my most:
Perhaps a monument of labor lost.
But thou, who givest all things, give not me
To sink in silence, seared with early cold,
Frost-burnt and blackened, but quick fire for frost!
As once I saw at a houseside, a tree
Struck scarlet by the lightning, utterly
To its last limb and twig: so strange it seemed,
I stopped to think if this indeed were May,
And were those windflowers? or had I dreamed?
But there it stood, close by the cottage eaves,
Red-ripened to the heart: shedding its leaves
And autumn sadness on the dim spring day.

HELEN HUNT JACKSON | 1830–1885

Crossed Threads

The silken threads by viewless spinners spun,
Which float so idly on the summer air,
And help to make each summer morning fair,
Shining like silver in the summer sun,
Are caught by wayward breezes, one by one,
And blown to east and west and fastened there,
Weaving on all the roads their sudden snare.
No sign which road doth safest, freest run,
The wingèd insects know, that soar so gay
To meet their death upon each summer day.
How dare we any human deed arraign;
Attempt to reckon any moment's cost;
Or any pathway trust as safe and plain
Because we see not where the threads have crossed?

The New Colossus

Not like the brazen giant of Greek fame,
With conquering limbs astride from land to land;
Here at our sea-washed, sunset gates shall stand
A mighty woman with a torch, whose flame
Is the imprisoned lightning, and her name
Mother of Exiles. From her beacon-hand
Glows world-wide welcome; her mild eyes command
The air-bridged harbor that twin cities frame.
"Keep, ancient lands, your storied pomp!" cries she
With silent lips. "Give me your tired, your poor,
Your huddled masses yearning to breathe free,
The wretched refuse of your teeming shore.
Send these, the homeless, tempest-tost to me,
I lift my lamp beside the golden door!"

Long Island Sound

I see it as it looked one afternoon
In August,—by a fresh soft breeze o'erblown.
The swiftness of the tide, the light thereon,
A far-off sail, white as a crescent moon.
The shining waters with pale currents strewn,
The quiet fishing-smacks, the Eastern cove,
The semi-circle of its dark, green grove.
The luminous grasses, and the merry sun
In the grave sky; the sparkle far and wide,
Laughter of unseen children, cheerful chirp
Of crickets, and low lisp of rippling tide,
Light summer clouds fantastical as sleep
Changing unnoted while I gazed thereon.
All these fair sounds and sights I made my own.

In Death Valley

There came gray stretches of volcanic plains,
Bare, lone and treeless, then a bleak lone hill,
Like to the dolorous hill that Dobell saw.
Around were heaps of ruins piled between
The Burn o' Sorrow and the Water o' Care;
And from the stillness of the down-crushed walls
One pillar rose up dark against the moon.
There was a nameless Presence everywhere;
In the gray soil there was a purple stain,
And the gray reticent rocks were dyed with blood—
Blood of a vast unknown Calamity.
It was the mark of some ancestral grief—
Grief that began before the ancient Flood.

LIZETTE WOODWORTH REESE | 1856–1935

April in Town

Straight from the east the wind blows sharp with rain,
  That just now drove its wild ranks down the street,
  And westward rushed into the sunset sweet.
Spouts brawl, boughs drip and cease and drip again,
Bricks gleam; keen saffron glows each window-pane,
  And every pool beneath the passing feet.
  Innumerable odors fine and fleet
Are blown this way from blossoming lawn and lane.
Wet roofs show black against a tender sky;
  The almond bushes in the lean-fenced square,
    Beaten to the walks, show all their draggled white.
A troop of laborers comes slowly by;
  One bears a daffodil, and seems to bear
    A new-lit candle through the fading light.

The Lights of London

The evenfall, so slow on hills, hath shot
Far down into the valley's cold extreme,
Untimely midnight; spire and roof and stream
Like fleeing spectres, shudder and are not.
The Hampstead hollies, from their sylvan plot
Yet cloudless, lean to watch as in a dream,
From chaos climb with many a sudden gleam,
London, one moment fallen and forgot.

Her booths begin to flare; and gases bright
Prick door and window; all her streets obscure
Sparkle and swarm with nothing true nor sure,
Full as a marsh of mist and winking light;
Heaven thickens over, Heaven that cannot cure
Her tear by day, her fevered smile by night.

GEORGE SANTAYANA | 1863–1952

FROM **Sonnets, 1883–1893**

III

O world, thou choosest not the better part!
It is not wisdom to be only wise,
And on the inward vision close the eyes,
But it is wisdom to believe the heart.
Columbus found a world, and had no chart,
Save one that faith deciphered in the skies;
To trust the soul's invincible surmise
Was all his science and his only art.
Our knowledge is a torch of smoky pine
That lights the pathway but one step ahead
Across a void of mystery and dread.
Bid, then, the tender light of faith to shine
By which alone the mortal heart is led
Unto the thinking of the thought divine.

XVI

A thousand beauties that have never been
Haunt me with hope and tempt me to pursue;
The gods, methinks, dwell just behind the blue;
The satyrs at my coming fled the green.
The flitting shadows of the grove between
The dryads' eyes were winking, and I knew
The wings of sacred Eros as he flew
And left me to the love of things not seen.
'Tis a sad love, like an eternal prayer,
And knows no keen delight, no faint surcease.
Yet from the seasons hath the earth increase,
And heaven shines as if the gods were there.
Had Dian passed there could no deeper peace
Embalm the purple stretches of the air.

II

With you a part of me hath passed away;
For in the peopled forest of my mind
A tree made leafless by this wintry wind
Shall never don again its green array.
Chapel and fireside, country road and bay,
Have something of their friendliness resigned;
Another, if I would, I could not find,
And I am grown much older in a day.
But yet I treasure in my memory
Your gift of charity, and young heart's ease,
And the dear honour of your amity;
For these once mine, my life is rich with these.
And I scarce know which part may greater be,—
What I keep of you, or you rob from me.

XXIX

What riches have you that you deem me poor,
Or what large comfort that you call me sad?
Tell me what makes you so exceeding glad:
Is your earth happy or your heaven sure?
I hope for heaven, since the stars endure
And bring such tidings as our fathers had.
I know no deeper doubt to make me mad,
I need no brighter love to keep me pure.
To me the faiths of old are daily bread;
I bless their hope, I bless their will to save,
And my deep heart still meaneth what they said.
It makes me happy that the soul is brave,
And, being so much kinsman to the dead,
I walk contented to the peopled grave.

RICHARD HOVEY | 1864–1900

Accident in Art

What painter has not with a careless smutch
Accomplished his despair?—one touch revealing
All he had put of life, thought, vigor, feeling,
Into the canvas that without that touch
Showed of his love and labor just so much
Raw pigment, scarce a scrap of soul concealing!
What poet has not found his spirit kneeling
A-sudden at the sound of such or such
Strange verses staring from his manuscript,
Written he knows not how, but which will sound
Like trumpets down the years? So Accident
Itself unmasks the likeness of Intent,
And ever in blind Chance's darkest crypt
The shrine-lamp of God's purposing is found.

EDWIN ARLINGTON ROBINSON | 1869–1935

Dear Friends

Dear friends, reproach me not for what I do,
Nor counsel me, nor pity me; nor say
That I am wearing half my life away
For bubble-work that only fools pursue.
And if my bubbles be too small for you,
Blow bigger then your own: the games we play
To fill the frittered minutes of a day,
Good glasses are to read the spirit through.

And whoso reads may get him some shrewd skill;
And some unprofitable scorn resign,
To praise the very thing that he deplores;
So, friends (dear friends), remember, if you will,
The shame I win for singing is all mine,
The gold I miss for dreaming is all yours.

Sonnet

Oh for a poet—for a beacon bright
To rift this changeless glimmer of dead gray;
To spirit back the Muses, long astray,
And flush Parnassus with a newer light;
To put these little sonnet-men to flight
Who fashion, in a shrewd mechanic way,
Songs without souls, that flicker for a day,
To vanish in irrevocable night.

What does it mean, this barren age of ours?
Here are the men, the women, and the flowers,
The seasons, and the sunset, as before.
What does it mean? Shall there not one arise
To wrench one banner from the western skies,
And mark it with his name forevermore?

The Clerks

I did not think that I should find them there
When I came back again; but there they stood,
As in the days they dreamed of when young blood
Was in their cheeks and women called them fair.
Be sure, they met me with an ancient air,—
And yes, there was a shop-worn brotherhood
About them; but the men were just as good,
And just as human as they ever were.

And you that ache so much to be sublime,
And you that feed yourselves with your descent,
What comes of all your visions and your fears?
Poets and kings are but the clerks of Time,
Tiering the same dull webs of discontent,
Clipping the same sad alnage of the years.

George Crabbe

Give him the darkest inch your shelf allows,
Hide him in lonely garrets, if you will,—
But his hard, human pulse is throbbing still
With the sure strength that fearless truth endows.
In spite of all fine science disavows,
Of his plain excellence and stubborn skill
There yet remains what fashion cannot kill,
Though years have thinned the laurel from his brows.

Whether or not we read him, we can feel
From time to time the vigor of his name
Against us like a finger for the shame
And emptiness of what our souls reveal
In books that are as altars where we kneel
To consecrate the flicker, not the flame.

On the Night of a Friend's Wedding

If ever I am old, and all alone,
I shall have killed one grief, at any rate;
For then, thank God, I shall not have to wait
Much longer for the sheaves that I have sown.
The devil only knows what I have done,
But here I am, and here are six or eight
Good friends, who most ingenuously prate
About my songs to such and such a one.

But everything is all askew to-night,—
As if the time were come, or almost come,
For their untenanted mirage of me
To lose itself and crumble out of sight,
Like a tall ship that floats above the foam
A little while, and then breaks utterly.

The Pity of the Leaves

Vengeful across the cold November moors,
Loud with ancestral shame there came the bleak
Sad wind that shrieked, and answered with a shriek,
Reverberant through lonely corridors.
The old man heard it; and he heard, perforce,
Words out of lips that were no more to speak—
Words of the past that shook the old man's cheek
Like dead, remembered footsteps on old floors.

And then there were the leaves that plagued him so!
The brown, thin leaves that on the stones outside
Skipped with a freezing whisper. Now and then
They stopped, and stayed there—just to let him know
How dead they were; but if the old man cried,
They fluttered off like withered souls of men.

L'Envoi

Now in a thought, now in a shadowed word,
Now in a voice that thrills eternity,
Ever there comes an onward phrase to me
Of some transcendent music I have heard;
No piteous thing by soft hands dulcimered,
No trumpet crash of blood-sick victory,
But a glad strain of some vast harmony
That no brief mortal touch has ever stirred.

There is no music in the world like this,
No character wherewith to set it down,
No kind of instrument to make it sing.
No kind of instrument? Ah, yes, there is;
And after time and place are overthrown,
God's touch will keep its one chord quivering.

Lost Anchors

Like a dry fish flung inland far from shore,
There lived a sailor, warped and ocean-browned,
Who told of an old vessel, harbor-drowned
And out of mind a century before,
Where divers, on descending to explore
A legend that had lived its way around
The world of ships, in the dark hulk had found
Anchors, which had been seized and seen no more.

Improving a dry leisure to invest
Their misadventure with a manifest
Analogy that he may read who runs,
The sailor made it old as ocean grass—
Telling of much that once had come to pass
With him, whose mother should have had no sons.

Many Are Called

The Lord Apollo, who has never died,
Still holds alone his immemorial reign,
Supreme in an impregnable domain
That with his magic he has fortified;
And though melodious multitudes have tried
In ecstasy, in anguish, and in vain,
With invocation sacred and profane
To lure him, even the loudest are outside.

Only at unconjectured intervals,
By will of him on whom no man may gaze,
By word of him whose law no man has read,
A questing light may rift the sullen walls,
To cling where mostly its infrequent rays
Fall golden on the patience of the dead.

The Sheaves

Where long the shadows of the wind had rolled,
Green wheat was yielding to the change assigned;
And as by some vast magic undivined
The world was turning slowly into gold.
Like nothing that was ever bought or sold
It waited there, the body and the mind;
And with a mighty meaning of a kind
That tells the more the more it is not told.

So in a land where all days are not fair,
Fair days went on till on another day
A thousand golden sheaves were lying there,
Shining and still, but not for long to stay—
As if a thousand girls with golden hair
Might rise from where they slept and go away.

II

There were long days when there was nothing said,
And there were longer nights when there was nought
But silence and recriminating thought
Between them like a field unharvested.
Antipathy was now their daily bread,
And pride the bitter drink they daily fought
To throw away. Release was all they sought
Of hope, colder than moonlight on the dead.

Wishing the other might at once be sure
And strong enough to shake the prison down,
Neither believed, although they strove together,
How long the stolid fabric would endure
That was a wall for them, and was to frown
And shine for them through many sorts of weather.

New England

Here where the wind is always north-north-east
And children learn to walk on frozen toes,
Wonder begets an envy of all those
Who boil elsewhere with such a lyric yeast
Of love that you will hear them at a feast
Where demons would appeal for some repose,
Still clamoring where the chalice overflows
And crying wildest who have drunk the least.

Passion is here a soilure of the wits,
We're told, and Love a cross for them to bear;
Joy shivers in the corner where she knits
And Conscience always has the rocking-chair,
Cheerful as when she tortured into fits
The first cat that was ever killed by Care.

Reunion

By some derision of wild circumstance
Not then our pleasure somehow to perceive,
Last night we fell together to achieve
A light eclipse of years. But the pale chance
Of youth resumed was lost. Time gave a glance
At each of us, and there was no reprieve;
And when there was at last a way to leave,
Farewell was a foreseen extravagance.

Tonight the west has yet a failing red,
While silence whispers of all things not here;
And round there where the fire was that is dead,
Dusk-hidden tenants that are chairs appear.
The same old stars will soon be overhead,
But not so friendly and not quite so near.

Into My Own

One of my wishes is that those dark trees,
So old and firm they scarcely show the breeze,
Were not, as 'twere, the merest mask of gloom,
But stretched away unto the edge of doom.

I should not be withheld but that some day
Into their vastness I should steal away,
Fearless of ever finding open land,
Or highway where the slow wheel pours the sand.

I do not see why I should e'er turn back,
Or those should not set forth upon my track
To overtake me, who should miss me here
And long to know if still I held them dear.

They would not find me changed from him they knew—
Only more sure of all I thought was true.

Mowing

There was never a sound beside the wood but one,
And that was my long scythe whispering to the ground.
What was it it whispered? I knew not well myself;
Perhaps it was something about the heat of the sun,
Something, perhaps, about the lack of sound—
And that was why it whispered and did not speak.
It was no dream of the gift of idle hours,
Or easy gold at the hand of fay or elf:
Anything more than the truth would have seemed
    too weak
To the earnest love that laid the swale in rows,
Not without feeble-pointed spikes of flowers
(Pale orchises), and scared a bright green snake.
The fact is the sweetest dream that labor knows.
My long scythe whispered and left the hay to make.

Meeting and Passing

As I went down the hill along the wall
There was a gate I had leaned at for the view
And had just turned from when I first saw you
As you came up the hill. We met. But all
We did that day was mingle great and small
Footprints in summer dust as if we drew
The figure of our being less than two
But more than one as yet. Your parasol
Pointed the decimal off with one deep thrust.
And all the time we talked you seemed to see
Something down there to smile at in the dust.
(Oh, it was without prejudice to me!)
Afterward I went past what you had passed
Before we met and you what I had passed.

The Oven Bird

There is a singer everyone has heard,
Loud, a mid-summer and a mid-wood bird,
Who makes the solid tree trunks sound again.
He says that leaves are old and that for flowers
Mid-summer is to spring as one to ten.
He says the early petal-fall is past
When pear and cherry bloom went down in showers
On sunny days a moment overcast;
And comes that other fall we name the fall.
He says the highway dust is over all.
The bird would cease and be as other birds
But that he knows in singing not to sing.
The question that he frames in all but words
Is what to make of a diminished thing.

Putting in the Seed

You come to fetch me from my work tonight
When supper's on the table, and we'll see
If I can leave off burying the white
Soft petals fallen from the apple tree
(Soft petals, yes, but not so barren quite,
Mingled with these, smooth bean and wrinkled pea;)
And go along with you ere you lose sight
Of what you came for and become like me,
Slave to a springtime passion for the earth.
How Love burns through the Putting in the Seed
On through the watching for that early birth
When, just as the soil tarnishes with weed,
The sturdy seedling with arched body comes
Shouldering its way and shedding the earth crumbs.

The Investment

Over back where they speak of life as staying
('You couldn't call it living, for it ain't'),
There was an old, old house renewed with paint,
And in it a piano loudly playing.

Out in the plowed ground in the cold a digger,
Among unearthed potatoes standing still,
Was counting winter dinners, one a hill,
With half an ear to the piano's vigor.

All that piano and new paint back there,
Was it some money suddenly come into?
Or some extravagance young love had been to?
Or old love on an impulse not to care—

Not to sink under being man and wife,
But get some color and music out of life?

The Master Speed

No speed of wind or water rushing by
But you have speed far greater. You can climb
Back up a stream of radiance to the sky,
And back through history up the stream of time.
And you were given this swiftness, not for haste
Nor chiefly that you may go where you will,
But in the rush of everything to waste,
That you may have the power of standing still—
Off any still or moving thing you say.
Two such as you with such a master speed
Cannot be parted nor be swept away
From one another once you are agreed
That life is only life forevermore
Together wing to wing and oar to oar.

Design

I found a dimpled spider, fat and white,
On a white heal-all, holding up a moth
Like a white piece of rigid satin cloth—
Assorted characters of death and blight
Mixed ready to begin the morning right,
Like the ingredients of a witches' broth—
A snow-drop spider, a flower like a froth,
And dead wings carried like a paper kite.

What had that flower to do with being white,
The wayside blue and innocent heal-all?
What brought the kindred spider to that height,
Then steered the white moth thither in the night?
What but design of darkness to appall?—
If design govern in a thing so small.

On a Bird Singing in Its Sleep

A bird half wakened in the lunar noon
Sang halfway through its little inborn tune.
Partly because it sang but once all night
And that from no especial bush's height;
Partly because it sang ventriloquist
And had the inspiration to desist
Almost before the prick of hostile ears,
It ventured less in peril than appears.
It could not have come down to us so far
Through the interstices of things ajar
On the long bead chain of repeated birth
To be a bird while we are men on earth
If singing out of sleep and dream that way
Had made it much more easily a prey.

Unharvested

A scent of ripeness from over a wall.
And come to leave the routine road
And look for what had made me stall,
There sure enough was an apple tree
That had eased itself of its summer load,
And of all but its trivial foliage free,
Now breathed as light as a lady's fan.
For there there had been an apple fall
As complete as the apple had given man.
The ground was one circle of solid red.

May something go always unharvested!
May much stay out of our stated plan,
Apples or something forgotten and left,
So smelling their sweetness would be no theft.

The Silken Tent

She is as in a field a silken tent
At midday when a sunny summer breeze
Has dried the dew and all its ropes relent,
So that in guys it gently sways at ease,
And its supporting central cedar pole,
That is its pinnacle to heavenward
And signifies the sureness of the soul,
Seems to owe naught to any single cord,
But strictly held by none, is loosely bound
By countless silken ties of love and thought
To everything on earth the compass round,
And only by one's going slightly taut
In the capriciousness of summer air
Is of the slightest bondage made aware.

Never Again Would Birds' Song Be the Same

He would declare and could himself believe
That the birds there in all the garden round
From having heard the daylong voice of Eve
Had added to their own an oversound,
Her tone of meaning but without the words.
Admittedly an eloquence so soft
Could only have had an influence on birds
When call or laughter carried it aloft.
Be that as may be, she was in their song.
Moreover her voice upon their voices crossed
Had now persisted in the woods so long
That probably it never would be lost.
Never again would birds' song be the same.
And to do that to birds was why she came.

——

Your image walks not in my common way.
Rarely I conjure up your face, recall
Your language, think to hear your footstep fall
In my lost home or see your eyes' sweet play.
Rather you share the life that sees not day,
Immured within the spirit's deep control,
Where thro' the tideless quiets of the soul
Your kingdom stretches far and far away.
For these our joys and griefs are less than we.
The deeper truths ask not our daily thought—
Their strength is peace, they know that we believe.
And whatsoever of sublime there be
Reaches and deepens and at last is wrought
Into that life we are but do not live.

———

Tho' lack of laurels and of wreaths not one
Prove you our lives abortive, shall we yet
Vaunt us our single aim, our hearts full set
To win the guerdon which is never won.
Witness, a purpose never is undone.
And tho' fate drain our seas of violet
To gather round our lives her wide-hung net,
Memories of hopes that are not shall atone.
Not wholly starless is the ill-starred life,
Not all is night in failure, and the shield
Sometimes well grasped, tho' shattered in the strife.
And here while all the lowering heaven is ringed
With our loud death-shouts echoed, on the field
Stands forth our Nikè, proud, tho' broken-winged.

Be still. The Hanging Gardens were a dream
That over Persian roses flew to kiss
The curlèd lashes of Semiramis.
Troy never was, nor green Skamander stream.
Provence and Troubadour are merest lies.
The glorious hair of Venice was a beam
Made within Titian's eye. The sunsets seem,
The world is very old and nothing is.
Be still. Thou foolish thing, thou canst not wake,
Nor thy tears wedge thy soldered lids apart,
But patter in the darkness of thy heart.
Thy brain is plagued. Thou art a frighted owl
Blind with the light of life thou'ldst not forsake,
And Error loves and nourishes thy soul.

———

Live blindly and upon the hour. The Lord,
Who was the Future, died full long ago.
Knowledge which is the Past is folly. Go,
Poor child, and be not to thyself abhorred.
Around thine earth sun-wingèd winds do blow
And planets roll; a meteor draws his sword;
The rainbow breaks his seven-coloured chord
And the long strips of river-silver flow:
Awake! Give thyself to the lovely hours.
Drinking their lips, catch thou the dream in flight
About their fragile hairs' aërial gold.
Thou art divine, thou livest,—as of old
Apollo springing naked to the light,
And all his island shivered into flowers.

―――

The melancholy year is dead with rain.
Drop after drop on every branch pursues.
From far away beyond the drizzled flues
A twilight saddens to the window pane.
And dimly thro' the chambers of the brain,
From place to place and gently touching, moves
My one and irrecoverable love's
Dear and lost shape one other time again.
So in the last of autumn for a day
Summer or summer's memory returns.
So in a mountain desolation burns
Some rich belated flower, and with the gray
Sick weather, in the world of rotting ferns
From out the dreadful stones it dies away.

Near Helikon

By such an all-embalming summer day
As sweetens now among the mountain pines
Down to the cornland yonder and the vines,
To where the sky and sea are mixed in gray,
How do all things together take their way
Harmonious to the harvest, bringing wines
And bread and light and whatsoe'er combines
In the large wreath to make it round and gay.
To me my troubled life doth now appear
Like scarce distinguishable summits hung
Around the blue horizon: places where
Not even a traveller purposeth to steer,—
Whereof a migrant bird in passing sung,
And the girl closed her window not to hear.

Autumn Refrain

The skreak and skritter of evening gone
And grackles gone and sorrows of the sun,
The sorrows of sun, too, gone . . . the moon and moon,
The yellow moon of words about the nightingale
In measureless measures, not a bird for me
But the name of a bird and the name of a nameless air
I have never—shall never hear. And yet beneath
The stillness of everything gone, and being still,
Being and sitting still, something resides,
Some skreaking and skrittering residuum,
And grates these evasions of the nightingale
Though I have never—shall never hear that bird.
And the stillness is in the key, all of it is,
The stillness is all in the key of that desolate sound.

Wild Peaches

I

When the world turns completely upside down
You say we'll emigrate to the Eastern Shore
Aboard a river-boat from Baltimore;
We'll live among wild peach trees, miles from town,
You'll wear a coonskin cap, and I a gown
Homespun, dyed butternut's dark gold colour.
Lost, like your lotus-eating ancestor,
We'll swim in milk and honey till we drown.

The winter will be short, the summer long,
The autumn amber-hued, sunny and hot,
Tasting of cider and of scuppernong;
All seasons sweet, but autumn best of all.
The squirrels in their silver fur will fall
Like falling leaves, like fruit, before your shot.

II

The autumn frosts will lie upon the grass
Like bloom on grapes of purple-brown and gold.
The misted early mornings will be cold;
The little puddles will be roofed with glass.
The sun, which burns from copper into brass,
Melts these at noon, and makes the boys unfold
Their knitted mufflers; full as they can hold,
Fat pockets dribble chestnuts as they pass.

Peaches grow wild, and pigs can live in clover;
A barrel of salted herrings lasts a year;
The spring begins before the winter's over.
By February you may find the skins
Of garter snakes and water moccasins
Dwindled and harsh, dead-white and cloudy-clear.

III

When April pours the colours of a shell
Upon the hills, when every little creek
Is shot with silver from the Chesapeake
In shoals new-minted by the ocean swell,
When strawberries go begging, and the sleek
Blue plums lie open to the blackbird's beak,
We shall live well—we shall live very well.

The months between the cherries and the peaches
Are brimming cornucopias which spill
Fruits red and purple, sombre-bloomed and black;
Then, down rich fields and frosty river beaches
We'll trample bright persimmons, while you kill
Bronze partridge, speckled quail, and canvasback.

IV

Down to the Puritan marrow of my bones
There's something in this richness that I hate.
I love the look, austere, immaculate,
Of landscapes drawn in pearly monotones.
There's something in my very blood that owns
Bare hills, cold silver on a sky of slate,
A thread of water, churned to milky spate
Streaming through slanted pastures fenced with stones.

I love those skies, thin blue or snowy gray,
Those fields sparse-planted, rendering meagre sheaves;
That spring, briefer than apple-blossom's breath,
Summer, so much too beautiful to stay,
Swift autumn, like a bonfire of leaves,
And sleepy winter, like the sleep of death.

Unfinished Portrait

My love, you know that I have never used
That fluency of colour smooth and rich
Could cage you in enamel for the niche
Whose heart-shape holds you; I have been accused
Of gold and silver trickery, infused
With blood of meteors, and moonstones which
Are cold as eyeballs in a flooded ditch;
In no such goblin smithy are you bruised.

I do not glaze a lantern like a shell
Inset with stars, nor make you visible
Through jewelled arabesques which adhere to clothe
The outline of your soul; I am content
To leave you an uncaptured element;
Water, or light, or air that's stained by both.

False Prophet

When I was forty, and two feathers sprung
Like crescents silver-curved from either temple,
Above a casque of bronze, I saw the simple
And casual shape of beauty; and my tongue
Spoke thus: "I am rejoiced I am not young
Lest this supreme and ultimate example
Of fine-spun flesh should very lightly trample
Upon my wounds; my withers are unwrung."

He might have been my son, save that my youth,
Bending the slender bow of its despair,
Loosed no such luminous arrow on the air;
His shaft was cut from some diviner bough:
And while my fainting heart perceived the truth,
My tongue spoke thus: "He cannot hurt me now."

Good Ships

Fleet ships encountering on the high seas
Who speak, and then unto the vast diverge,
Two hailed each other, poised on the loud surge
Of one of Mrs. Grundy's Tuesday teas,
Nor trimmed one sail to baffle the driving breeze.
A macaroon absorbed all her emotion;
His hue was ruddy but an effect of ocean;
They exchanged the nautical technicalities.

It was only a nothing or so until they parted.
Away they went, most certainly bound for port,
So seaworthy one felt they could not sink;
Still there was a tremor shook them, I should think,
Beautiful timbers fit for storm and sport
And unto miserly merchant hulks converted.

Parting at Dawn

If there was a broken whispering by night
It was an image of the coward heart,
But the white dawn assures them how to part—
Stoics are born on the cold glitter of light
And with the morning star lovers take flight.
Say then your parting; and most dry should you drain
Your lips of the wine, your eyes of the frantic rain,
Till these be as the barren anchorite.

And then? O dear Sir, stumbling down the street,
Continue, till you come to wars and wounds;
Beat the air, Madam, till your house-clock sounds;
And if no Lethe flows beneath your casement,
And when ten years have not brought full effacement,
Philosophy was wrong, and you may meet.

Piazza Piece

—I am a gentleman in a dustcoat trying
To make you hear. Your ears are soft and small
And listen to an old man not at all,
They want the young men's whispering and sighing.
But see the roses on your trellis dying
And hear the spectral singing of the moon;
For I must have my lovely lady soon,
I am a gentleman in a dustcoat trying.

—I am a lady young in beauty waiting
Until my truelove comes, and then we kiss.
But what grey man among the vines is this
Whose words are dry and faint as in a dream?
Back from my trellis, Sir, before I scream!
I am a lady young in beauty waiting.

FROM *And in the Human Heart*

X

If we must speak, then let us humbly speak;
humbly becomes the great, and great we are;
ice is the silent language of the peak;
and fire the silent language of the star;
the sun is silent, the moon silent, too—
only the wind gives voice to ice or flame;
let us be modest, then, of I and You,
and give them back the hugeness whence they came.
Shadow to you, the subtle—light to me,
the nimble—and the twilight soul between,
in which, embracing, we may learn to be,
and having learned to be, may learn to mean;
then we shall speak, as the moon speaks, with snow,
our words already frozen, long ago.

XXXIX

Bird's eye or snake's eye, bright through leaves; the leaf
inscribed by sun with an all-cryptic message;
downflash of raindrop, no less slight and brief
than these; or snake or bird in soundless passage;
or as the cloud's rim, golden against the moon,
golden and bronze, swimming like foam to vanish,
fire-phosphor seethed on sand, and gone as soon,
immortal light to burnish or replenish;
one secret shape of cloud; one look; one mark
hurriedly notched on the all-hurrying sun;
bird's eye and snake's eye seen; then instant dark;
but not before the unplumbed world there known:
how swiftly turn the pages of this book,
whose secrets flash and vanish, even as we look!

CLAUDE McKAY | 1889-1948

Dawn in New York

The Dawn! The Dawn! The crimson-tinted, comes
Out of the low still skies, over the hills,
Manhattan's roofs and spires and cheerless domes!
The Dawn! My spirit to its spirit thrills.
Almost the mighty city is asleep,
No pushing crowd, no tramping, tramping feet.
But here and there a few cars groaning creep
Along, above, and underneath the street,
Bearing their strangely-ghostly burdens by,
The women and the men of garish nights,
Their eyes wine-weakened and their clothes awry,
Grotesques beneath the strong electric lights.
The shadows wane. The Dawn comes to New York.
And I go darkly-rebel to my work.

Outcast

For the dim regions whence my fathers came
My spirit, bondaged by the body, longs.
Words felt, but never heard, my lips would frame;
My soul would sing forgotten jungle songs.
I would go back to darkness and to peace,
But the great western world holds me in fee,
And I may never hope for full release
While to its alien gods I bend my knee.
Something in me is lost, forever lost,
Some vital thing has gone out of my heart,
And I must walk the way of life a ghost
Among the sons of earth, a thing apart;
For I was born, far from my native clime,
Under the white man's menace, out of time.

———

If I should learn, in some quite casual way,
That you were gone, not to return again—
Read from the back-page of a paper, say,
Held by a neighbor in a subway train,
How at the corner of this avenue
And such a street (so are the papers filled)
A hurrying man, who happened to be you,
At noon today had happened to be killed—
I should not cry aloud—I could not cry
Aloud, or wring my hands in such a place—
I should but watch the station lights rush by
With a more careful interest on my face;
Or raise my eyes and read with greater care
Where to store furs and how to treat the hair.

—

I think I should have loved you presently,
And given in earnest words I flung in jest;
And lifted honest eyes for you to see,
And caught your hand against my cheek and breast;
And all my pretty follies flung aside
That won you to me, and beneath your gaze,
Naked of reticence and shorn of pride,
Spread like a chart my little wicked ways.
I, that had been to you, had you remained,
But one more waking from a recurrent dream,
Cherish no less the certain stakes I gained,
And walk your memory's halls, austere, supreme,
A ghost in marble of a girl you knew
Who would have loved you in a day or two.

——

I shall forget you presently, my dear,
So make the most of this, your little day,
Your little month, your little half a year,
Ere I forget, or die, or move away,
And we are done forever; by and by
I shall forget you, as I said, but now,
If you entreat me with your loveliest lie
I will protest you with my favourite vow.
I would indeed that love were longer-lived,
And oaths were not so brittle as they are,
But so it is, and nature has contrived
To struggle on without a break thus far,—
Whether or not we find what we are seeking
Is idle, biologically speaking.

Love is not blind. I see with single eye
Your ugliness and other women's grace.
I know the imperfection of your face,—
The eyes too wide apart, the brow too high
For beauty. Learned from earliest youth am I
In loveliness, and cannot so erase
Its letters from my mind, that I may trace
You faultless, I must love until I die.
More subtle is the sovereignty of love:
So am I caught that when I say, "Not fair,"
'Tis but as if I said, "Not here—not there—
Not risen—not writing letters." Well I know
What is this beauty men are babbling of;
I wonder only why they prize it so.

Oh, oh, you will be sorry for that word!
Give back my book and take my kiss instead.
Was it my enemy or my friend I heard,
"What a big book for such a little head!"
Come, I will show you now my newest hat,
And you may watch me purse my mouth and prink!
Oh, I shall love you still, and all of that.
I never again shall tell you what I think.
I shall be sweet and crafty, soft and sly;
You will not catch me reading any more:
I shall be called a wife to pattern by;
And some day when you knock and push the door,
Some sane day, not too bright and not too stormy,
I shall be gone, and you may whistle for me.

Sonnet to Gath

Country of hunchbacks!—where the strong,
    straight spine,
Jeered at by crooked children, makes his way
Through by-streets at the kindest hour of day,
Till he deplore his stature, and incline
To measure manhood with a gibbous line;
Till out of loneliness, being flawed with clay,
He stoop into his neighbour's house and say,
"Your roof is low for me—the fault is mine."
Dust in an urn long since, dispersed and dead
Is great Apollo; and the happier he;
Since who amongst you all would lift a head
At a god's radiance on the mean door-tree,
Saving to run and hide your dates and bread,
And cluck your children in about your knee?

VII

Night is my sister, and how deep in love,
How drowned in love and weedily washed ashore,
There to be fretted by the drag and shove
At the tide's edge, I lie—these things and more:
Whose arm alone between me and the sand,
Whose voice alone, whose pitiful breath brought near,
Could thaw these nostrils and unlock this hand,
She could advise you, should you care to hear.
Small chance, however, in a storm so black,
A man will leave his friendly fire and snug
For a drowned woman's sake, and bring her back
To drip and scatter shells upon the rug.
No one but Night, with tears on her dark face,
Watches beside me in this windy place.

XXXIII

Sorrowful dreams remembered after waking
Shadow with dolour all the candid day;
Even as I read, the silly tears out-breaking
Splash on my hands and shut the page away. . . .
Grief at the root, a dark and secret dolour,
Harder to bear than wind-and-weather grief,
Clutching the rose, draining its cheek of colour,
Drying the bud, curling the opened leaf.
Deep is the pond—although the edge be shallow,
Frank in the sun, revealing fish and stone,
Climbing ashore to turtle-head and mallow—
Black at the centre beats a heart unknown.
Desolate dreams pursue me out of sleep;
Weeping I wake; waking, I weep, I weep.

XXXV

Clearly my ruined garden as it stood
Before the frost came on it I recall—
Stiff marigolds, and what a trunk of wood
The zinnia had, that was the first to fall;
These pale and oozy stalks, these hanging leaves
Nerveless and darkened, dripping in the sun,
Cannot gainsay me, though the spirit grieves
And wrings its hands at what the frost has done.
If in a widening silence you should guess
I read the moment with recording eyes,
Taking your love and all your loveliness
Into a listening body hushed of sighs . . .
Though summer's rife and the warm rose in season,
Rebuke me not: I have a winter reason.

XLVI

Even in the moment of our earliest kiss,
When sighed the straitened bud into the flower,
Sat the dry seed of most unwelcome this;
And that I knew, though not the day and hour.
Too season-wise am I, being country-bred,
To tilt at autumn or defy the frost:
Snuffing the chill even as my fathers did,
I say with them, "What's out tonight is lost."
I only hoped, with the mild hope of all
Who watch the leaf take shape upon the tree,
A fairer summer and a later fall
Than in these parts a man is apt to see,
And sunny clusters ripened for the wine:
I tell you this across the blackened vine.

—

I too beneath your moon, almighty Sex,
Go forth at nightfall crying like a cat,
Leaving the lofty tower I laboured at
For birds to foul and boys and girls to vex
With tittering chalk; and you, and the long necks
Of neighbours sitting where their mothers sat
Are well aware of shadowy this and that
In me, that's neither noble nor complex.
Such as I am, however, I have brought
To what it is, this tower; it is my own;
Though it was reared To Beauty, it was wrought
From what I had to build with: honest bone
Is there, and anguish; pride; and burning thought;
And lust is there, and nights not spent alone.

SAMUEL GREENBERG | 1893–1917

FROM **Sonnets of Apology**

XXVII. Immortality

But only to be memories of spiritual gate,
Letting us feel the difference from the real;
Are not limits the sooth to formulate
Theories thereof, simply our ruler to feel?
Basques of statuettes of eruptions long ago,
Of power in symmetry, marvel of thought
The crafts attempt, showing rare aspiration;
The museums of the ancient fine stones
For bowls and cups found historians
Sacred adorations, the numismatist hath shown,
But only to be memories of spiritual gate,
Letting us feel the difference from the real;
Are not limits the sooth to formulate
Theories thereof, simply our ruler to feel?

E. E. CUMMINGS | 1894–1962

----

a wind has blown the rain away and blown
the sky away and all the leaves away,
and the trees stand.   I think i too have known
autumn too long

                    (and what have you to say,
wind wind wind—did you love somebody
and have you the petal of somewhere in your heart
pinched from dumb summer?
                            O crazy daddy
of death dance cruelly for us and start

the last leaf whirling in the final brain
of air!)Let us as we have seen see
doom's integration.........a wind has blown the rain

away and the leaves and the sky and the
trees stand:
            the trees stand.   The trees,
suddenly wait against the moon's face.

———

"next to of course god america i
love you land of the pilgrims' and so forth oh
say can you see by the dawn's early my
country 'tis of centuries come and go
and are no more what of it we should worry
in every language even deafanddumb
thy sons acclaim your glorious name by gorry
by jingo by gee by gosh by gum
why talk of beauty what could be more beaut-
iful than these heroic happy dead
who rushed like lions to the roaring slaughter
they did not stop to think they died instead
then shall the voice of liberty be mute?"

He spoke.   And drank rapidly a glass of water

——

if i have made,my lady,intricate
imperfect various things chiefly which wrong
your eyes(frailer than most deep dreams are frail)
songs less firm than your body's whitest song
upon my mind—if i have failed to snare
the glance too shy—if through my singing slips
the very skilful strangeness of your smile
the keen primeval silence of your hair

—let the world say "his most wise music stole
nothing from death"—
                          you only will create
(who are so perfectly alive)my shame:
lady through whose profound and fragile lips
the sweet small clumsy feet of April came

into the ragged meadow of my soul.

——

he does not have to feel because he thinks
(the thoughts of others,be it understood)
he does not have to think because he knows
(that anything is bad which you think good)

because he knows,he cannot understand
(why Jones don't pay me what he knows he owes)
because he cannot understand,he drinks
(and he drinks and he drinks and he drinks and)

not bald.   (Coughs.)   Two pale slippery small eyes

balanced upon one broken babypout
(pretty teeth wander into which and out
of)Life,dost Thou contain a marvel than
this death named Smith less strange?

                              Married and lies

afraid;aggressive and:American

———

pity this busy monster,manunkind,

not.   Progress is a comfortable disease:
your victim(death and life safely beyond)

plays with the bigness of his littleness
—electrons deify one razorblade
into a mountainrange;lenses extend

unwish through curving wherewhen till unwish
returns on its unself.
                              A world of made
is not a world of born—pity poor flesh

and trees,poor stars and stones,but never this
fine specimen of hypermagical

ultraomnipotence.   We doctors know

a hopeless case if—listen:there's a hell
of a good universe next door;let's go

———

why must itself up every of a park

anus stick some quote statue unquote to
prove that a hero equals any jerk
who was afraid to dare to answer "no"?

quote citizens unquote might otherwise
forget(to err is human;to forgive
divine)that if the quote state unquote says
"kill" killing is an act of christian love.

"Nothing" in 1944 AD

"can stand against the argument of mil
itary necessity"(generalissimo e)
and echo answers "there is no appeal

from reason"(freud)—you pays your money and
you doesn't take your choice.   Ain't freedom grand

—

from spiralling ecstatically this

proud nowhere of earth's most prodigious night
blossoms a newborn babe:around him,eyes
—gifted with every keener appetite
than mere unmiracle can quite appease—
humbly in their imagined bodies kneel
(over time space doom dream while floats the whole

perhapsless mystery of paradise)

mind without soul may blast some universe
to might have been,and stop ten thousand stars
but not one heartbeat of this child;nor shall
even prevail a million questionings
against the silence of his mother's smile

—whose only secret all creation sings

—

all worlds have halfsight,seeing either with

life's eye(which is if things seem spirits)or
(if spirits in the guise of things appear)
death's:any world must always half perceive.

Only whose vision can create the whole

(being forever born a foolishwise
proudhumble citizen of ecstasies
more steep than climb can time with all his years)

he's free into the beauty of the truth;

and strolls the axis of the universe
—love.   Each believing world denies,whereas
your lover(looking through both life and death)
timelessly celebrates the merciful

wonder no world deny may or believe

FROM **On Drink**

II

Strong drink goes to the soul and sets it free
Of its reserve, and dignity dissolves,
For drink corrodes that bright machinery
In which the educated soul revolves.

The soul with wings is but a hopeful lie
Until there comes a sudden magic bath
Of bottled fire, which by its alchemy
Creates us pinions for a dizzy path.

And then the soul, an eaglet swiftly grown,
Plays with a drunken brother in the clouds,
Or by itself, serenely and alone,
It balances above the sober crowds.

Do not forget, young eagles, that you must,
But for this drink, have been forever dust.

Sonnet

Since you would claim the sources of my thought
Recall the meshes whence it sprang unlimed,
The reedy traps which other hands have timed
To close upon it. Conjure up the hot
Blaze that it cleared so cleanly, or the snow
Devised to strike it down. It will be free.
Whatever nets draw in to prison me
At length your eyes must turn to watch it go.

My mouth, perhaps, may learn one thing too well,
My body hear no echo save its own,
Yet will the desperate mind, maddened and proud,
Seek out the storm, escape the bitter spell
That we obey, strain to the wind, be thrown
Straight to its freedom in the thunderous cloud.

Simple Autumnal

The measured blood beats out the year's delay.
The tearless eyes and heart, forbidden grief,
Watch the burned, restless, but abiding leaf,
The brighter branches arming the bright day.

The cone, the curving fruit should fall away,
The vine stem crumble, ripe grain know its sheaf.
Bonded to time, fires should have done, be brief,
But, serfs to sleep, they glitter and they stay.

Because not last nor first, grief in its prime
Wakes in the day, and hears of life's intent.
Sorrow would break the seal stamped over time
And set the baskets where the bough is bent.

Full season's come, yet filled trees keep the sky
And never scent the ground where they must lie.

Single Sonnet

Now, you great stanza, you heroic mould,
Bend to my will, for I must give you love:
The weight in the heart that breathes, but cannot move,
Which to endure flesh only makes so bold.

Take up, take up, as it were lead or gold
The burden; test the dreadful mass thereof.
No stone, slate, metal under or above
Earth, is so ponderous, so dull, so cold.

Too long as ocean bed bears up the ocean,
As earth's core bears the earth, have I borne this;
Too long have lovers, bending for their kiss,
Felt bitter force cohering without motion.

Staunch meter, great song, it is yours, at length,
To prove how stronger you are than my strength.

JOHN WHEELWRIGHT | 1897–1940

FROM **Mirrors of Venus**

VII. Sanct

We know the Love the Father bears the Son
is a third Mask and that the Three form One.
We also know, machines and dynamos
—Preservers in motion; Destroyers in repose—
like visions of wheeled eyes the addict sees
are gods, not fashioned in our images.

Thus let us state the unknown in the known:
The mechanism of our friendship, grown
transcendent over us, maintains a being
by seeing us when we grow lax in seeing,
although without our sight it could not be.
(One states, one does not solve, a mystery.)
This human Trinity is comprehended
when doubt of its divinity has ended.

XII. Mother

Dame Nature is no less a snob than we
for she discriminates between her friends,
imposing variously for varied ends
the limits on her wide benignity.
In her, not our own kindly mother see;
but, rather, a strange hostess, who unbends
upon occasion, occasionally sends
her invitations,—"quite informally."

I do not mean to cast, hereby, reflection
on the Darwinian Theory of Selection;
nor to ridicule the Pathetic Fallacy;
but only to point out the different status,
the obvious, intellectual hiatus
between snobbism by fresh ponds, and by a sea.

XIII. Father

An East Wind asperges Boston with Lynn's sulphurous
    brine.
Under the bridge of turrets my father built,—from
    turning sign
of CHEVROLET, out-topping our gilt State House dome
to burning sign of CARTER'S INK,—drip multitudes
of checker-board shadows. Inverted turreted reflections
sleeting over axle-grease billows, through all directions
cross-cut parliamentary gulls, who toss like gourds.

    Speak. Speak to me again, as fresh saddle leather
    (speak; talk again) to a hunter smells of heather.
    Come home. Wire a wire of warning without words.
    Come home and talk to me again, my first friend.
        Father,
    come home, dead man, who made your mind my
        home.

XXIX. Phallus

Friends need not guard each other as a jealous
Moslem must segregate his odalisque,
no more than one need see the symboled phallus
while meditating at an obelisk.
　　If we could be together day after day,
　　companionship, pointed with entering wedge
　　compact, whittled by common task and play
　　inevitable and slow, would split the pledge
　　which kisses tallied once in valediction:
　　that our hidden selves in separation meet.
　　The corollary's simple contradiction
　　may render yet the contract obsolete.
Habit is evil,—all habit, even speech;
and promises prefigure their own breach.

Twilight of the Wood

Leaf is no more now than corruption's scent
But beautiful are the trees above their dead,
This hour with their summer beauties spent,
When desolate of the thousand sweets they shed,
As to that last and western rite made bare,
Their boughs let drop the amber-yielding cup
That leaves no stain upon the crystal air;
And thinly in their midst a tune goes up:
Then who might sing in all the muted wood?
Its waters locked, no single bird, no leaf;
It is not higher than the living blood
Will sound in bodies stony-dull with grief;
And thus, when death has taken all the rest,
Life's self is heard within earth's icy breast.

Alas, Kind Element!

Then I was sealed, and like the wintering tree
I stood me locked upon a summer core;
Living, had died a death, and asked no more.
And I lived then, but as enduringly,
And my heart beat, but only as to be.
Ill weathers well, hail, gust and cold I bore,
I held my life as hid, at root, in store:
Thus I lived then, till this air breathed on me.
Till this kind air breathed kindness everywhere,
There where my times had left me I would stay.
Then I was staunch, I knew nor yes nor no;
But now the wishful leaves have thronged the air.
My every leaf leans forth upon the day;
Alas, kind element! which comes to go.

To Emily Dickinson

You who desired so much—in vain to ask—
Yet fed your hunger like an endless task,
Dared dignify the labor, bless the quest—
Achieved that stillness ultimately best,

Being, of all, least sought for: Emily, hear!
O sweet, dead Silencer, most suddenly clear
When singing that Eternity possessed
And plundered momently in every breast;

—Truly no flower yet withers in your hand.
The harvest you descried and understand
Needs more than wit to gather, love to bind.
Some reconcilement of remotest mind—

Leaves Ormus rubyless, and Ophir chill.
Else tears heap all within one clay-cold hill.

ALLEN TATE | 1899–1979

The Subway

Dark accurate plunger down the successive knell
Of arch on arch, where ogives burst a red
Reverberance of hail upon the dead
Thunder like an exploding crucible!
Harshly articulate, musical steel shell
Of angry worship, hurled religiously
Upon your business of humility
Into the iron forestries of hell:

Till broken in the shift of quieter
Dense altitudes tangential of your steel,
I am become geometries, and glut
Expansions like a blind astronomer
Dazed, while the worldless heavens bulge and reel
In the cold revery of an idiot.

FROM **Sonnets at Christmas**

II

Ah, Christ, I love you rings to the wild sky
And I must think a little of the past:
When I was ten I told a stinking lie
That got a black boy whipped; but now at last
The going years, caught in an after-glow,
Reverse like balls englished upon green baize—
Let them return, let the round trumpets blow
The ancient crackle of the Christ's deep gaze.
Deafened and blind, with senses yet unfound,
Am I, untutored to the after-wit
Of knowledge, knowing a nightmare has no sound;
Therefore with idle hands and head I sit
In late December before the fire's daze
Punished by crimes of which I would be quit.

To the memory of Denis Devlin

II

The day's at end and there's nowhere to go,
Draw to the fire, even this fire is dying;
Get up and once again politely lying
Invite the ladies toward the mistletoe
With greedy eyes that stare like an old crow.
How pleasantly the holly wreaths did hang
And how stuffed Santa did his reindeer clang
Above the golden oaken mantel, years ago!

Then hang this picture for a calendar,
As sheep for goat, and pray most fixedly
For the cold martial progress of your star,
With thoughts of commerce and society,
Well-milked Chinese, Negroes who cannot sing,
The Huns gelded and feeding in a ring.

The Prince

The prince or statesman who would rise to power
Must rise through shallow trickery, and speak
The tongue of knavery, deceive the hour,
Use the corrupt, and still corrupt the weak.

And he who having power would serve the State,
Must now deceive corruption unto good,
By indirection strengthen love with hate,
Must love mankind with craft and hardihood:

Betray the witless unto wisdom, trick
Disaster to good luck, escape the gaze
Of all the pure at heart, each lunatic
Of innocence, who draws you to his daze:

And this frail balance to immortalize,
Stare publicly from death through marble eyes.

R. P. BLACKMUR | 1904–1965

Phasellus Ille

This little boat you see, my friends, has not,
as once Catullus' pinnance could repeat,
a history of deep-sea peril sought;
for her no honoured peace, no earned retreat.
Too narrow for her length in beam, unstable
and unseaworthy, her strakes and transom leak;
although no landsman, even, would call her able,
I float her daily in our tidal creek.

I do not need the bluster and the wail
in this small boat, of perilous high seas
nor the blown salt smarting in my teeth;
if the tide lift and weigh me in his scale
I know, and feel in me the knowledge freeze,
how smooth the utter sea is, underneath.

II. Wind and Weather

The heart exaggerates. I have not lost
despite the wind and weather, no, nor shall,
more than the heart must lose, no more at most
than when a thief cries thief, no more at all.
What can be shared seems never a full share
until by justifiable grand theft
each in his guilt has tenderness to spare.
Only of what I stole am I bereft.

That which was once, is now again my own.
It was my own affection stolen back
that seemed so sweet, the known returned unknown;
I gave that I might measure my own lack,
she hers. The rest was social wind and weather:
the storm that forced still holds our lives together.

RICHARD EBERHART | 1904–2005

Burden

Whoever lives beside a mountain knows,
Although he dares not speak it out, that he
Must always carry on his heart the snows
That burden down the trees. And never the sea
Will rush around him cool, like snow-cool air,
And carry him and lift him like a leaf.
He will not find this lightness anywhere
Since mountains brood, they hold dark league with grief.

The pine trees never tire of moving down
The slopes to meet him, pointing up from town
Beyond the tree-line to the rigid peaks.
The mountain holds him though it never speaks.
He scrambles over boulders on his knees
Trying to reach the summit, like the trees.

Petit Jour

A cold light for orisons. Reflect
Upon the diver ascending fathoms five.
Rumple the newest skull and genuflect.
Father, since our scholastic members thrive,
May we compel this world for clasp of thee,
Seeing, as morning flares and night's imagined
Mist dries from the air like memory,
The sun's transparent basin licked by wind.
Therein be instruments fittingly strung
To sound the enviable surf aloud,
While we whose business is not old nor young
Compose in winter light the winter cloud,
Returning when thy creative interval
Has taken down the evening from the wall.

Sonnet

Caught—the bubble
in the spirit-level,
a creature divided;
and the compass needle
wobbling and wavering,
undecided.
Freed—the broken
thermometer's mercury
running away;
and the rainbow-bird
from the narrow bevel
of the empty mirror,
flying wherever
it feels like, gay!

J. V. CUNNINGHAM | 1911–1985

The Aged Lover Discourses in the Flat Style

There are, perhaps, whom passion gives a grace,
Who fuse and part as dancers on the stage,
But that is not for me, not at my age,
Not with my bony shoulders and fat face.
Yet in my clumsiness I found a place
And use for passion: with it I ignore
My gaucheries and yours, and feel no more
The awkwardness of the absurd embrace.

It is a pact men make, and seal in flesh,
To be so busy with their own desires
Their loves may be as busy with their own,
And not in union. Though the two enmesh
Like gears in motion, each with each conspires
To be at once together and alone.

The Beautiful American Word, Sure

The beautiful American word, Sure,
As I have come into a room, and touch
The lamp's button, and the light blooms with such
Certainty where the darkness loomed before,

As I care for what I do not know, and care
Knowing for little she might not have been,
And for how little she would be unseen,
The intercourse of lives miraculous and dear.

Where the light is, and each thing clear,
Separate from all others, standing in its place,
I drink the time and touch whatever's near,

And hope for day when the whole world has that face:
For what assures her present every year?
In dark accidents the mind's sufficient grace.

KARL SHAPIRO | 1913–2000

Christmas Eve: Australia

The wind blows hot. English and foreign birds
And insects different as their fish excite
The would-be calm. The usual flocks and herds
Parade in permanent quiet out of sight,
And there one crystal like a grain of light
Sticks in the crucible of day and cools.
A cloud burnt to a crisp at some great height
Sips at the dark condensing in deep pools.

I smoke and read my Bible and chew gum,
Thinking of Christ and Christmas of last year,
And what those quizzical soldiers standing near
Ask of the war and Christmases to come,
And sick of causes and the tremendous blame
Curse lightly and pronounce your serious name.

Full Moon: New Guinea

These nights we fear the aspects of the moon,
Sleep lightly in the radiance falling clear
On palms and ferns and hills and us; for soon
The small burr of the bombers in our ear
Tickles our rest; we rise as from a nap
And take our helmets absently and meet,
Prepared for any spectacle or mishap,
At trenches fresh and narrow at our feet.

Look up, look up, and wait and breathe. These nights
We fear Orion and the Cross. The crowd
Of deadly insects caught in our long lights
Glitter and seek to burrow in a cloud
Soft-minded with high explosive. Breathe and wait,
The bombs are falling darkly for our fate.

JOHN BERRYMAN | 1914–1972

FROM **Berryman's Sonnets**

XI

I expect you from the North. The path winds in
Between the honeysuckle and the pines, among
Poison ivy and small flowerless shrubs,
Across the red-brown needle-bed. I sit
Or smoking pace. A moment since, at six,
Mist wrapped the knoll, but now birds like a gong
Beat, greet the white-gold level shine. Wide-flung
On a thousand greens the late slight rain is gleaming.

A rabbit jumps a shrub. O my quick darling,
Lie torpid so? Cars from the highway whine,
Dawn's trunks against the sun are black. I shiver.
Your hair this fresh wind would—but I am starting.
To what end does this easy and crystal light
Dream on the flat leaves, emerald, and shimmer? . .

WELDON KEES | 1914–1955

To Build a Quiet City in His Mind

To build a quiet city in his mind:
A single overwhelming wish; to build,
Not hastily, for there is so much wind,
So many eager smilers to be killed,
Obstructions one might overlook in haste:
The ruined structures cluttering the past,

A little at a time and slow is best,
Crawling as though through endless corridors,
Remembering always there are many doors
That open to admit the captured guest
Once only.
               Yet in spite of loss and guilt
And hurricanes of time, it might be built:

A refuge, permanent, with trees that shade
When all the other cities die and fade.

ROBERT LOWELL | 1917–1977

The North Sea Undertaker's Complaint

Now south and south and south the mallard heads,
His green-blue bony hood echoes the green
Flats of the Weser, and the mussel beds
Are sluggish where the webbed feet spanked the lean
Eel grass to tinder in the take-off. South
Is what I think of. It seems yesterday
I slid my hearse across the river mouth
And pitched the first iced mouse into the hay.
Thirty below it is. I hear our dumb
Club-footed orphan ring the Angelus
And clank the bell-chain for St. Gertrude's choir
To wail with the dead bell the martyrdom
Of one more blue-lipped priest; the phosphorous
Melted the hammer of his heart to fire.

Inauguration Day: January 1953

The snow had buried Stuyvesant.
The subways drummed the vaults. I heard
the El's green girders charge on Third,
Manhattan's truss of adamant,
that groaned in ermine, slummed on want. . . .
Cyclonic zero of the word,
God of our armies, who interred
Cold Harbor's blue immortals, Grant!
Horseman, your sword is in the groove!

Ice, ice. Our wheels no longer move.
Look, the fixed stars, all just alike
as lack-land atoms, split apart,
and the Republic summons Ike,
the mausoleum in her heart.

WILLIAM MEREDITH | 1919–2007

The Illiterate

Touching your goodness, I am like a man
Who turns a letter over in his hand
And you might think this was because the hand
Was unfamiliar but, truth is, the man
Has never had a letter from anyone;
And now he is both afraid of what it means
And ashamed because he has no other means
To find out what it says than to ask someone.

His uncle could have left the farm to him,
Or his parents died before he sent them word,
Or the dark girl changed and want him for beloved.
Afraid and letter-proud, he keeps it with him.
What would you call his feeling for the words
That keep him rich and orphaned and beloved?

This Present Past

The tulip's cup falls open helplessly,
The redbud's petals are already dust,
The trees are dropping all their various dreck
Pertaining to generation; once again
The spring has gone, as we complain it does
Year after year, before we had the time
To take it in.
            But brief as flowering
Has always been, our power to attend
Is briefer by far, and intermittent, too.
We look at the iris, say how beautiful,
And look no more, nor watch the fail and fall
Of its bruised flags. So runs the world away,
As blown about upon the rainy wind
The keys of the maple's kingdom copter down.

A Miltonic Sonnet for Mr. Johnson
on His Refusal of Peter Hurd's Official Portrait

Heir to the office of a man not dead
Who drew our Declaration up, who planned
Range and Rotunda with his drawing-hand
And harbored Palestrina in his head,
Who would have wept to see small nations dread
The imposition of our cattle-brand,
With public truth at home mistold or banned,
And in whose term no army's blood was shed,

Rightly you say the picture is too large
Which Peter Hurd by your appointment drew,
And justly call that Capitol too bright
Which signifies our people in your charge;
Wait, Sir, and see how time will render you,
Who talk of vision but are weak of sight.

6 January 1967

ANTHONY HECHT | 1923–2004

Fifth Avenue Parade

Vitrines of pearly gowns, bright porcelains,
Gilded dalmatics, the stone balconies
Of eminence, past all of these and past
The ghostly conquerors in swirls of bronze,
The children's pond, the Rospigliosi Cup,
Prinked with the glitter of day, the chrome batons
Of six high-stepping, slick drum-majorettes,
A local high school band in Robin's Egg Blue,
Envied by doormen, strippers, pianists,
Frogged with emblazonments, all smiles, advance
With victorious booms and fifings through a crowd
Flecked with balloons and flags and popsicles
Toward some weak, outnumbered, cowering North
That will lay down its arms at Eighty-sixth.

Summer Storm

In that so sudden summer storm they tried
Each bed, couch, closet, carpet, car-seat, table,
Both river banks, five fields, a mountain side,
Covering as much ground as they were able.

A lady, coming on them in the dark
In a white fixture, wrote to the newspapers
Complaining of the statues in the park.
By Cupid, but they cut some pretty capers!

The envious oxen in still rings would stand
Ruminating. Their sweet incessant plows
I think had changed the contours of the land
And made two modest conies move their house.

God rest them well, and firmly shut the door.
Now they are married Nature breathes once more.

The Virgin Mary

The hovering and huge, dark, formless sway
That nature moves by laws we contemplate
We name for lack of name as order, fate,
God, principle, or primum mobile.
But in that graven image, word made wood
By skillful faith of him to whom she was
Eternal nature, first and final cause,
The form of knowledge knowledge understood
Bound human thought against the dark we find.
And body took the image of the mind
To shape in chaos a congruent form
Of will and matter, equal, side by side,
Upon the act of faith, within the norm
Of carnal being, blind and glorified.

The Astronomers of Mont Blanc

Who are you there that, from your icy tower,
Explore the colder distances, the far
Escape of your whole universe to night;
That watch the moon's blue craters, shadowy crust,
And blunted mountains mildly drift and glare,
Ballooned in ghostly earnest on your sight;
Who are you, and what hope persuades your trust?

It is your hope that you will know the end
And compass of our ignorant restraint
There in lost time, where what was done is done
Forever as a havoc overhead.
Aging, you search to master in the faint
Persistent fortune which you gaze upon
The perfect order trusted to the dead.

The Poet at Seven

And on the porch, across the upturned chair,
The boy would spread a dingy counterpane
Against the length and majesty of the rain,
And on all fours crawl in it like a bear,
To lick his wounds in secret, in his lair;
And afterward, in the windy yard again,
One hand cocked back, release his paper plane,
Frail as a mayfly to the faithless air.
And summer evenings he would spin around
Faster and faster till the drunken ground
Rose up to meet him; sometimes he would squat
Among the foul weeds of the vacant lot,
Waiting for dusk and someone dear to come
And whip him down the street, but gently, home.

The Artist Orpheus

It was a tropical landscape, much like Florida's, which
    he knew.
(Childhood came blazing back at him.) They glided
    across a black
And apathetic river which reflected nothing back
Except his own face sinking gradually from view
As in a fading photograph.
                    Not that he meant to stay,
But, yes, he *would* play something for them, played Ravel;
And sang; and for the first time there were tears in hell.
(Sunset continued. Years passed, or a day.)
And the shades relented finally and seemed sorry.
He could have sworn then he did not look back,
That no one had been following on his track,
Only the thing was that it made a better story
To say that he had heard a sigh perhaps
And once or twice the sound a twig makes when it snaps.

Marsyas

I used to write in the café sometimes:
Poems on menus, read all over town
Or talked out before ever written down.
One day a girl brought in his latest book.
I opened it—stiff rhythms, gorgeous rhymes—
And made a face. Then crash! my cup upset.
Of twenty upward looks mine only met
His, that gold archaic lion's look

Wherein I saw my wiry person skinned
Of every skill it labored to acquire
And heard the plucked nerve's elemental twang.
They found me dangling where his golden wind
Inflicted so much music on the lyre
That no one could have told you what he sang.

The Broken Home

Crossing the street,
I saw the parents and the child
At their window, gleaming like fruit
With evening's mild gold leaf.

In a room on the floor below,
Sunless, cooler—a brimming
Saucer of wax, marbly and dim—
I have lit what's left of my life.

I have thrown out yesterday's milk
And opened a book of maxims.
The flame quickens. The word stirs.

Tell me, tongue of fire,
That you and I are as real
At least as the people upstairs.

My father, who had flown in World War I,
Might have continued to invest his life
In cloud banks well above Wall Street and wife.
But the race was run below, and the point was to win.

Too late now, I make out in his blue gaze
(Through the smoked glass of being thirty-six)
The soul eclipsed by twin black pupils, sex
And business; time was money in those days.

Each thirteenth year he married. When he died
There were already several chilled wives
In sable orbit—rings, cars, permanent waves.
We'd felt him warming up for a green bride.

He could afford it. He was "in his prime"
At three score ten. But money was not time.

When my parents were younger this was a popular act:
A veiled woman would leap from an electric, wine-dark
    car
To the steps of no matter what—the Senate or the Ritz
    Bar—
And bodily, at newsreel speed, attack

No matter whom—Al Smith or José Maria Sert
Or Clemenceau—veins standing out on her throat
As she yelled *War mongerer! Pig! Give us the vote!*,
And would have to be hauled away in her hobble skirt.

What had the man done? Oh, made history.
Her business (he had implied) was giving birth,
Tending the house, mending the socks.

Always that same old story—
Father Time and Mother Earth,
A marriage on the rocks.

One afternoon, red, satyr-thighed
Michael, the Irish setter, head
Passionately lowered, led
The child I was to a shut door. Inside,

Blinds beat sun from the bed.
The green-gold room throbbed like a bruise.
Under a sheet, clad in taboos
Lay whom we sought, her hair undone, outspread,

And of a blackness found, if ever now, in old
Engravings where the acid bit.
I must have needed to touch it
Or the whiteness—was she dead?
Her eyes flew open, startled strange and cold.
The dog slumped to the floor. She reached for me. I fled.

Tonight they have stepped out onto the gravel.
The party is over. It's the fall
Of 1931. They love each other still.

She: Charlie, I can't stand the pace.
He: Come on, honey—why, you'll bury us all!

A lead soldier guards my windowsill:
Khaki rifle, uniform, and face.
Something in me grows heavy, silvery, pliable.

How intensely people used to feel!
Like metal poured at the close of a proletarian novel,
Refined and glowing from the crucible,
I see those two hearts, I'm afraid,
Still. Cool here in the graveyard of good and evil,
They are even so to be honored and obeyed.

. . . Obeyed, at least, inversely. Thus
I rarely buy a newspaper, or vote.
To do so, I have learned, is to invite
The tread of a stone guest within my house.

Shooting this rusted bolt, though, against him,
I trust I am no less time's child than some
Who on the heath impersonate Poor Tom
Or on the barricades risk life and limb.

Nor do I try to keep a garden, only
An avocado in a glass of water—
Roots pallid, gemmed with air. And later,

When the small gilt leaves have grown
Fleshy and green, I let them die, yes, yes,
And start another. I am earth's no less.

A child, a red dog roam the corridors,
Still, of the broken home. No sound. The brilliant
Rag runners halt before the wide-open doors.
My old room! Its wallpaper—cream, medallioned
With pink and brown—brings back the first nightmares,
Long summer colds, and Emma, sepia-faced,
Perspiring over broth carried upstairs
Aswim with golden fats I could not taste.

The real house became a boarding school.
Under the ballroom ceiling's allegory
Someone at last may actually be allowed
To learn something; or, from my window, cool
With the unstiflement of the entire story,
Watch a red setter stretch and sink in cloud.

Saint Judas

When I went out to kill myself, I caught
A pack of hoodlums beating up a man.
Running to spare his suffering, I forgot
My name, my number, how my day began,
How soldiers milled around the garden stone
And sang amusing songs; how all that day
Their javelins measured crowds; how I alone
Bargained the proper coins, and slipped away.

Banished from heaven, I found this victim beaten,
Stripped, kneed, and left to cry. Dropping my rope
Aside, I ran, ignored the uniforms:
Then I remembered bread my flesh had eaten,
The kiss that ate my flesh. Flayed without hope,
I held the man for nothing in my arms.

Jefferson Valley

The tops of the spruces here have always done
Ragged things to the skies arranged behind them
Like slates at twilight; and the morning sun
Has marked out trees and hedgerows, and defined them
In various greens, until, toward night, they blur
Back into one rough palisade again,
Furred thick with dusk. No wind we know can stir
This olive blackness that surrounds us when
It becomes the boundary of what we know
By limiting the edge of what we see.
When sunlight shows several spruces in a row,
To know the green of a particular tree
 Means disbelief in darkness; and the lack
 Of a singular green is what we mean by black.

ADRIENNE RICH | b. 1929

The Insusceptibles

Then the long sunlight lying on the sea
Fell, folded gold on gold; and slowly we
Took up our decks of cards, our parasols,
The picnic hamper and the sandblown shawls
And climbed the dunes in silence. There were two
Who lagged behind as lovers sometimes do,
And took a different road. For us the night
Was final, and by artificial light
We came indoors to sleep. No envy there
Of those who might be watching anywhere
The lustres of the summer dark, to trace
Some vagrant splinter blazing out of space.
No thought of them, save in a lower room
To leave a light for them when they should come.

ROBERT MEZEY | b. 1935

Owl

Nightlong waiting and listening, being schooled
To long lying awake without thoughts,
I hear him calling from the other world.
A long silence, and then two flutey notes—
The cry of nobody, but urgent, cool,
Full of foreboding. He's in the cedar tree
Not twenty feet beyond my window sill;
The other world is very far away.
When, towards morning, he ceases, the air seems
More visible, although it's not yet light,
The black sky drained and all our speechless dreams
Fading into thought. Lord of the night,
Thy kingdom in which everything is one,
Come, speak to me, speak to me once again.

SOURCES AND ACKNOWLEDGMENTS

NOTES

INDEX OF POETS,
TITLES, AND FIRST LINES

SOURCES AND
ACKNOWLEDGMENTS

John Quincy Adams, "To the Sun-Dial," *Poems of Religion and Society, by John Quincy Adams, with Notices of His Life and Character by John Davis and T. H. Benton* (New York: William H. Graham, 1848).

Léonie Adams, "Twilight of the Wood," *Those Not Elect* (New York: Robert M. McBride & Co., 1925); "Alas, Kind Element!" *Poems: A Selection* (New York: Funk & Wagnalls, 1954). Both reprinted from *Poems: A Selection*, by permission of Judith Farr, Literary Executrix of Léonie Adams Estate.

Conrad Aiken, Sonnets X and XXXIX, *And in the Human Heart* (New York: Duell, Sloan & Pearce, 1940). Both reprinted from *Collected Poems: Second Edition* (New York: Oxford University Press, 1970). Copyright © 1940, 1968 by Conrad Aiken. Reprinted by permission of Brandt & Hochman Literary Agents, Inc.

Washington Allston, "On the Luxembourg Gallery," *The Sylphs of the Seasons, with Other Poems* (London: W. Pople, 1813). Reprinted from *Lectures on Art, and Poems*, edited by Richard Henry Dana, Jr. (New York: Baker & Scribner, 1850).

John Berryman, Sonnet XI, *Berryman's Sonnets* (New York: Farrar, Straus & Giroux, 1967). Copyright © 1967 by John Berryman. Copyright renewed © 1995 by Kate Berryman. Reprinted by permission of Farrar, Straus and Giroux, LLC.

Elizabeth Bishop, "Sonnet," *The Complete Poems 1927–1979* (New York: Farrar, Straus & Giroux, 1983). Copyright 1979, 1983 by Alice Helen Methfessel. Reprinted by permission of Farrar, Straus and Giroux, LLC.

R. P. Blackmur, "Phasellus Ille," and "Wind and Weather" *from* "Dedications," *From Jordan's Delight* (New York: Arrow Editions, 1937). Both reprinted from *Poems of R. P. Blackmur* (Princeton, N.J.: Princeton University Press, 1977). Copyright © 1977 by Princeton University Press, renewed 2005 by Princeton University Press. Reprinted by permission of the publisher.

Louise Bogan, "Sonnet," *Body of This Death* (New York: Robert M. McBride & Co., 1923); "Simple Autumnal," *Dark Summer* (New York: Charles Scribner's Sons, 1929); "Single Sonnet," *The Sleeping Fury* (New York: Charles Scribner's Sons, 1937). All reprinted from *The Blue Estuaries: Poems 1923–1968* (New York: Farrar, Straus & Giroux, 1968). Copyright © 1968 by Louise Bogan. Copyright renewed by Ruth Limmer. Reprinted by permission of Farrar, Straus and Giroux, LLC.

Edgar Bowers, "The Virgin Mary," *The Form of Loss* (Denver: Alan Swallow, 1956); "The Astronomers of Mont Blanc," *The Astronomers* (Denver: Alan Swallow, 1965). Both reprinted from *Collected Poems* (New York: Alfred A. Knopf, 1997). Copyright © 1997 by Edgar Bowers. Used by permission of Alfred A. Knopf, a division of Random House, Inc.

William Cullen Bryant, "November" and "To an American Painter Departing for Europe," *Poems* (New York: E. Bliss, 1832).

Hart Crane, "To Emily Dickinson," *from* the unfinished book "Key West: An Island Sheaf," *The Collected Poems of Hart Crane*, edited by Waldo Frank (New York: Liveright, 1933). Reprinted from *The Poems of Hart Crane*, edited by Marc Simon (New York: Liveright, 1986). Copyright © 1933, 1958, 1966 by Liveright Publishing Corporation. Copyright © 1986 by Marc Simon. Used by permission of Liveright Publishing Corporation.

E. E. Cummings, "a wind has blown the rain away and blown," *Tulips and Chimneys* (New York: Thomas Seltzer, 1923); " 'next to of course god america i" and "if I have made,my lady,intricate," *is 5* (New York: Boni & Liveright, 1926); "he does not have to feel because he thinks," *Collected Poems* (New York: Harcourt, Brace & Co., 1938); "pity this busy monster,manunkind," *1 x 1* (New York: Henry Holt & Co., 1944); "why must itself up every of a park," *XAIPE* (New York: Oxford University Press, 1950); "from spiralling ecstatically this," *95 Poems* (New York: Harcourt, Brace & Co., 1958); "all worlds have halfsight,seeing either with," *73 Poems* (New York: Harcourt, Brace & World, 1963). All reprinted from *Complete Poems 1904–1962*, edited by George J. Firmage (New York: Liveright, 1991). Copyright © 1923, 1925, 1926, 1931, 1935, 1938, 1939, 1940, 1944, 1945, 1946, 1947, 1948, 1949, 1950, 1951, 1952, 1953, 1954, 1955, 1956, 1957, 1958, 1959, 1960, 1961, 1962, 1963, 1966, 1967, 1968, 1972, 1973, 1974, 1975, 1976, 1977, 1978, 1979, 1980, 1981, 1982, 1983, 1984, 1985, 1986, 1987, 1988, 1989, 1990, 1991 by the Trustees for the E. E. Cummings Trust. Copyright © 1973, 1976, 1978, 1979, 1981, 1983, 1985, 1991 by George James Firmage. Used by permission of Liveright Publishing Corporation.

Donald Justice, "The Poet at Seven," *The Summer Anniversaries* (Middletown, Conn.: Wesleyan University Press, 1960); "The Artist Orpheus," *New and Selected Poems* (New York: Alfred A. Knopf, 1995). Both reprinted from *Collected Poems* (New York: Alfred A. Knopf, 2004). Copyright © 2004 by Donald Justice. Used by permission of Alfred A. Knopf, a division of Random House, Inc.

Weldon Kees, "To Build a Quiet City in His Mind," *The Collected Poems of Weldon Kees*, edited by Donald Justice (Iowa City: Stone Wall Press, 1960). Reprinted from *The Collected Poems of Weldon Kees: Revised Edition*, edited by Donald Justice (Lincoln: University of Nebraska Press, 1975). Copyright © 1962, 1965, renewed 2003 by the University of Nebraska Press. Reprinted by permission of the University of Nebraska Press.

Emma Lazarus, "The New Colossus" and "Long Island Sound," *The Poems of Emma Lazarus*, edited by Mary Lazarus and Annie Lazarus (Boston & New York: Houghton, Mifflin & Co., 1889).

Henry Wadsworth Longfellow, *from* "Divina Commedia," *The Inferno of Dante Alighieri* (Boston: privately published, 1865); "The Sound of the Sea," *The Masque of Pandora and Other Poems* (Boston: James R. Osgood & Co., 1875); "Nature" and "The Harvest Moon," *Kéramos and Other Poems* (Boston: Houghton, Osgood & Co., 1878); "Mezzo Cammin" and "The Cross of Snow," *The Life of Henry Wadsworth Longfellow, with Extracts from His Journals and Correspondence*, by Samuel Longfellow (Boston: Ticknor & Fields, 1886). All reprinted from *The Writings of Henry Wadsworth Longfellow, with Bibliographical and Critical Notes*, edited by Horace E. Scudder (Boston & New York: Houghton, Mifflin & Co., 1886).

James Russell Lowell, "The Street," *Poems* (Cambridge, Mass.: John Owen, 1844).

Robert Lowell, "The North Sea Undertaker's Complaint," *Lord Weary's Castle* (New York: Harcourt, Brace & Co., 1946) Copyright © 1946, renewed 1974 by Robert Lowell. Reprinted by permission of Harcourt, Inc.; "Inauguration Day: January 1953," *Life Studies* (New York: Farrar, Straus & Cudahy, 1959). Both reprinted from *Collected Poems*, edited by Frank Bidart and David Gewanter (New York: Farrar, Straus & Giroux, 2003). Copyright © 2003 by Harriet Lowell and Sheridan Lowell. Reprinted by permission of Farrar, Straus and Giroux, LLC.

Edwin Markham, "In Death Valley," *The Man with the Hoe and Other Poems* (New York: Doubleday & McClure Co., 1899).

Claude McKay, "Dawn in New York" and *Outcast," *Harlem Shadows: The Poems of Claude McKay* (New York: Harcourt, Brace & Co., 1922). Both reprinted from *Claude McKay: Complete Poems*, edited by William Jay Maxwell (Urbana & Chicago: University of Illinois Press, 2003). Reprinted courtesy of the Literary Representative for the Works of Claude McKay, Schomburg Center for Research in Black Culture, The New York Public Library, Astor, Lenox and Tilden Foundations.

William Meredith, "The Illiterate," *The Open Sea and Other Poems* (New York: Alfred A. Knopf, 1958). Reprinted from *Effort at Speech: New and Selected Poems* (Evanston, Ill.: TriQuarterly Books / Northwestern University Press, 1997). Copyright © 1997 by William Meredith. All rights reserved; used by permission of Northwestern University Press and the author.

James Merrill, "Marsyas," *The Country of a Thousand Years of Peace* (New York: Alfred A. Knopf, 1959); "The Broken Home," *Nights and Days* (New York: Atheneum, 1966). Both reprinted from *Collected Poems*, edited by J. D. McClatchy and Stephen Yenser (New York: Alfred A. Knopf, 2001). Copyright © 2001 by the Literary Estate of James Merrill at Washington University. Used by permission of Alfred A. Knopf, a division of Random House, Inc.

Robert Mezey, "Owl," *Evening Wind and Other Poems* (Middletown, Conn.: Wesleyan University Press, 1987). Reprinted from *Collected Poems 1952–1999* (Fayetteville: University of Arkansas Press, 2000). Copyright © 2000 by Robert Mezey. Reprinted with permission of the University of Arkansas Press, www.uapress.com.

Edna St. Vincent Millay, "If I should learn, in some quite casual way," *Renascence and Other Poems* (New York: Mitchell Kennerley, 1917); "I think I should have loved you presently" and "I shall forget you presently, my dear," *A Few Figs from Thistles* (New York: Frank Shay, 1920); "Love is not blind. I see with single eye" and "Oh, oh, you will be sorry for that word!" *The Harp-Weaver and Other Poems* (New York: Harper & Bros., 1923); "Sonnet to Gath," *The Buck in the Snow and Other Poems* (New York: Harper & Bros., 1928); Sonnets VII, XXXIII, XXXV, and XLVI, *Fatal Interview* (New York: Harper & Bros., 1931); "I too beneath your moon, almighty Sex," *Huntsman, What Quarry?* (New York: Harper & Bros., 1939). All reprinted from *Collected Poems*, edited by Norma Millay (New York: Harper & Row, 1956). Copyright © 1923, 1928, 1931, 1939 by Edna St. Vincent Millay, renewed © 1951, 1955, 1958, 1967 by Norma Millay Ellis. Reprinted by permission of the Edna St. Vincent Millay Society.

Howard Nemerov, "This Present Past," *Inside the Onion* (Chicago: University of Chicago Press, 1984). Reprinted from *Trying Conclusions: New and Selected Poems 1961–1991* (Chicago: University of Chicago Press, 1991). Copyright © 1991 by The University of Chicago. Reprinted by permission of Margaret Nemerov.

Edgar Allan Poe, "To Science," *Al Aaraaf, Tamerlane, and Minor Poems* (Baltimore: Hatch & Dunning, 1829). Reprinted from *The Raven and Other Poems* (New York: Wiley & Putnam, 1845).

H. Phelps Putnam, *from* "On Drink," *Trinc* (New York: George H. Doran, 1927). Reprinted from *The Collected Poems of H. Phelps Putnam*, edited by Charles R. Walker (New York: Farrar, Straus & Giroux, 1971). Copyright

John Crowe Ransom, "Good Ships" and "Parting at Dawn," *Chills and Fever* (New York: Alfred A. Knopf, 1924); "Piazza Piece," *Two Gentlemen in Bonds* (New York: Alfred A. Knopf, 1927). All reprinted from *Selected Poems: Third Edition, Revised and Enlarged* (New York: Alfred A. Knopf, 1964). Copyright © 1924, 1927 by Alfred A. Knopf, Inc. and renewed 1952, 1955 by John Crowe Ransom. Used by permission of Alfred A. Knopf, a division of Random House, Inc.

Lizette Woodworth Reese, "April in Town," *A Handful of Lavender* (Boston & New York: Houghton, Mifflin & Co., 1891).

Adrienne Rich, "The Insusceptibles," *The Diamond Cutters and Other Poems* (New York: Harper & Bros., 1955). Reprinted from *Collected Early Poems 1950–1970* (New York: W. W. Norton, 1993). Copyright © 1993, 1955 by Adrienne Rich. Used by permission of W. W. Norton & Company, Inc.

Edwin Arlington Robinson, "Dear Friends," "Sonnet," "The Clerks," "George Crabbe," and "On the Night of a Friend's Wedding," *The Torrent and The Night Before* (Cambridge, Mass.: privately printed, 1896); "The Pity of the Leaves" and "L'Envoi," *The Children of the Night* (Boston: Richard G. Badger & Co., 1897); "Lost Anchors" and "Many Are Called," *Avon's Harvest* (New York: Macmillan, 1921); "The Sheaves," *from* "Not Always," "New England," and "Reunion," *Dionysus in Doubt* (New York: Macmillan, 1925). All reprinted from *Collected Poems of Edwin Arlington Robinson: Complete Edition with Additional Poems* (New York: Macmillan, 1937). Copyright © 1937. Reprinted with the permission of Scribner, an imprint of Simon & Schuster Adult Publishing Group.

George Santayana, Sonnets III and XVI *from* "Sonnets, 1883–1893" (I–XX) and Sonnet II *from* "To W. P.," *Sonnets and Other Verses* (Cambridge, Mass. & Chicago: Stone & Kimball, 1894); Sonnet XXIX *from* "Sonnets, 1895" (XXI–L), *Sonnets and Other Verses*, enlarged edition (New York: Stone & Kimball, 1896). All reprinted from *The Complete Poems of George Santayana: A Critical Edition*, edited by William G. Holzberger (Lewisburg, Pa.: Bucknell University Press, 1979). Reprinted with permission.

Delmore Schwartz, "The Beautiful American Word, Sure," *In Dreams Begin Responsibilities* (Norfolk, Conn.: New Directions, 1938). Reprinted from *Selected Poems 1938–1959: Summer Knowledge* (Garden City: Doubleday, 1959). Copyright © 1959 by Delmore Schwartz. Reprinted by permission of New Directions Publishing Corp.

Karl Shapiro, "Christmas Eve: Australia" and "Full Moon: New Guinea," *V-Letter and Other Poems* (New York: Reynal & Hitchcock, 1944). Both reprinted from *Collected Poems 1940–1978* (New York: Random House, 1978). Copyright © 1943, 1971 by Karl Shapiro. Reprinted by permission of Harold Ober & Associates.

Louis Simpson, "Summer Storm," *The Arrivistes: Poems 1940–1949* (New York: The Fine Editions Press, 1949). Reprinted from *The Owner of the*

House: New Collected Poems 1940–2001 (Rochester, N.Y.: BOA Editions, Ltd., 2003). Copyright © 2003 by Louis Simpson. Reprinted with the permission of BOA Editions, Ltd.

Wallace Stevens, "Autumn Refrain," *Ideas of Order* (New York: The Alcestis Press, 1935). Reprinted from *The Collected Poems of Wallace Stevens* (New York: Alfred A. Knopf, 1954). Copyright © 1954 by Wallace Stevens and renewed 1982 by Holly Stevens. Used by permission of Alfred A. Knopf, a division of Random House, Inc.

Trumbull Stickney, "Your image walks not in my common way," "Tho' lack of laurels and of wreaths not one," "Be still. The Hanging Gardens were a dream," "Live blindly and upon the hour. The Lord," "The melancholy year is dead with rain," and "Near Helikon," *The Poems of Trumbull Stickney*, edited by George Cabot Lodge, William Vaughn Moody, and John Ellerton Lodge (Boston & New York: Houghton, Mifflin & Co., 1905). All reprinted from *The Poems of Trumbull Stickney*, edited by Amberys R. Whittle (New York: Farrar, Straus & Giroux, 1972). Copyright © 1972 Amberys R. Whittle. Reprinted by permission of Farrar, Straus and Giroux, LLC.

Allen Tate, "The Subway," *Mr. Pope and Other Poems* (New York: Minton, Balch & Co., 1928); Sonnet II *from* "Sonnets at Christmas," *Selected Poems* (New York: Charles Scribner's Sons, 1937); Sonnet II *from* "More Sonnets at Christmas," *Poems 1922–1947* (New York: Charles Scribner's Sons, 1948). All reprinted from *Collected Poems 1919–1976* (New York: Farrar, Straus & Giroux, 1977). Copyright © 1977 by Allen Tate. Reprinted by permission of Farrar, Straus and Giroux, LLC.

Henry David Thoreau, "This is my Carnac, whose unmeasured dome," *A Week on the Concord and Merrimack Rivers* (Boston: James Munroe & Co., 1849). Reprinted from the "New and Revised" second edition (Boston: Ticknor & Fields, 1868).

Frederick Goddard Tuckerman, Sonnets VII, X, and XXVIII of "Sonnets, First Series" and Sonnets VII, XV, XVI, XVIII, XXIX, XXX, and XXXII of "Sonnets, Second Series," *Poems* (Boston: John Wilson & Son, 1860); Sonnets IV, VI, VII, IX, and X of "Sonnets, Third Series," Sonnets I and VIII of "Sonnets, Fourth Series," and Sonnets III and XVI of "Sonnets, Fifth Series," *Sonnets of Frederick Goddard Tuckerman*, edited by Witter Bynner (New York: Alfred A. Knopf, 1931). All reprinted from *The Complete Poems of Frederick Goddard Tuckerman*, edited by N. Scott Momaday (New York: Oxford University Press, 1965). Copyright © 1965 by Oxford University Press, Inc. Reprinted by permission of Oxford University Press, Inc.

Jones Very, "The Columbine," "The New Birth," "The Garden," "The Latter Rain," "The Dead," "Thy Brother's Blood," and "Nature," *Essays and Poems*, edited by Ralph Waldo Emerson (Boston: C. C. Little & J. Brown, 1839); "The Barberry Bush," *Parnassus*, edited by Ralph Waldo Emerson (Boston & New York: Houghton, Mifflin & Co., 1874); "Autumn

Leaves," "The Hand and Foot," "Yourself," and "The Lost," *Poems of Jones Very*, edited by William P. Andrews (Boston & New York: Houghton, Mifflin & Co., 1883); "The Children" and *from* "The Origin of Man," *Poems and Essays by Jones Very: Complete and Revised Edition*, edited by James Freeman Clarke (Boston & New York: Houghton, Mifflin & Co., 1886). All reprinted from *Jones Very: The Complete Poems*, edited by Helen R. Deese (Athens: University of Georgia Press, 1993). Copyright © 1993 by Helen R. Deese. Reprinted with permission.

John Wheelwright, "Sanct," "Mother," "Father," and "Phallus," *Mirrors of Venus: A Novel in Sonnets* (Boston: Bruce Humphries, 1938). All reprinted from *The Collected Poems of John Wheelwright*, edited by Alvin H. Rosenfeld (New York: New Directions, 1972). Copyright © 1971 by John Wheelwright. Reprinted by permission of New Directions Publishing Corp.

Richard Wilbur, "A Miltonic Sonnet for Mr. Johnson on His Refusal of Peter Hurd's Official Portrait," *Walking to Sleep: New Poems and Translations* (Harcourt, Brace & World, 1969). Reprinted from *Collected Poems 1943–2004* (New York & San Diego: Harcourt, Inc., 2004) Copyright © 1967 by Richard Wilbur. Reprinted by permission of Harcourt, Inc.

Yvor Winters, "The Prince," *Before Disaster* (Tryon, N.C.: Tryon Pamphlets, 1934). Reprinted from *The Selected Poems of Yvor Winters*, edited by R. L. Barth (Athens, Ohio: Swallow Press / Ohio University Press, 1999). Copyright © 1927, 1930, 1931, 1934, 1937, 1940, 1943, 1950, 1952, 1960, 1966 by Yvor Winters. Reprinted by permission of Ohio University Press/Swallow Press, Athens, Ohio.

James Wright, "Saint Judas," *Saint Judas* (Middletown, Conn.: Wesleyan University Press, 1959). Reprinted from *Above the River: The Complete Poems* (New York: Farrar, Straus & Giroux and University Press of New England, 1990). Copyright © 1959 by James Wright. Reprinted by permission of Wesleyan University Press.

Elinor Wylie, "Wild Peaches," *Nets to Catch the Wind* (New York: Harcourt, Brace & Co., 1921); "Unfinished Portrait," *Black Armour* (New York: George H. Doran, 1923); "False Prophet," *Trivial Breath* (New York: Alfred A. Knopf, 1928). All reprinted from *Collected Poems of Elinor Wylie* (New York: Alfred A. Knopf, 1932).

This volume presents the texts of the original printings chosen for inclusion here, but it does not attempt to reproduce nontextual features of their typographic design. The texts are presented without change, except for the correction of typographical errors. Spelling, punctuation, and capitalization are often expressive features and are not altered, even when inconsistent or irregular. The following typographical errors have been corrected (cited by page and line number): 1.10, moontide; 22.1, and the Foot; 31.16, walls; 59.3, changless; 129.12, (Speak; 130.13, May.

NOTES

2.2   Luxembourg Gallery]   The Palais du Luxembourg was the Paris home of Marie de' Medici after the death of her husband, Henry IV. In 1622, Peter Paul Rubens (1577–1640) accepted her commission to furnish the palace's gallery with 24 large allegorical canvases depicting scenes from her life, most of which now hang in the Louvre.

4.3   Cole!]   Thomas Cole (1801–1848) was known as the founder of the Hudson River School of landscape painting. He was a friend of Bryant, who wrote this sonnet in 1829 shortly before Cole left the States for a four-year study tour of England, France, and Italy.

5.2   Mezzo Cammin]   Cf. Dante, *Inferno*, Canto 1, line 1: *Nel mezzo del cammin di nostra vita* ("Midway upon the journey of our life"). Longfellow wrote this sonnet at Boppard on the Rhine, on August 25, 1842, when he was 35. It was published posthumously, in his brother Samuel's *Life of Henry Wadsworth Longfellow, with Extracts from His Journals and Correspondence* (1886).

6.1   *Divina Commedia*]   Longfellow published this sonnet as a preface to his translation of Dante's *Inferno*, privately printed in Boston in 1865. It was later incorporated into *Divina Commedia*, a sequence of six sonnets published in his collection *Flower-de-Luce* (1866).

10.1   The Cross of Snow]   Longfellow wrote this sonnet on July 10, 1879, the 18th anniversary of the death of his second wife, Fanny, after her dress caught fire in a freak domestic accident. It was published posthumously, in the *Life of Henry Wadsworth Longfellow* (1886).

10.10   a mountain in the distant West]   The Mount of the Holy Cross, west of Vail, Colorado, in the Northern Sawatch Range, is noted for its east-facing couloir, which forms a well-defined Latin cross that is visible for miles.

11.2   To Science]   Cf. Keats's "Lamia" (1819), especially Part II, lines 234–37: "Philosophy will clip an Angel's wings, / Conquer all mysteries by rule and line, / Empty the haunted air, and gnomed mine— / Unweave a rainbow." When this sonnet, first published in 1829, was reprinted in *The Raven and Other Poems* (1845), Poe described it in a footnote as one of "the crude compositions of my earliest boyhood."

15.1   The Latter Rain]   Cf. Zechariah 10:1 and James 5:7.

17.1   Thy Brother's Blood]   See Genesis 4:1–15.

19.1   The Children]   Cf. 1 Corinthians 8.

23.4–5   For thou beneath the earth . . . walks upon;]   Cf. Luke 11:44.

25.1   *The Origin of Man*]   A pair of thematically linked sonnets, first collected in the 1886 edition of Very's *Poems and Essays*.

26.3   This is my Carnac,]   In *A Week on the Concord and Merrimack Rivers*, Thoreau prefaces this sonnet with the following comment: "Our own country furnishes antiquities as ancient and durable, and as useful, as any. . . . What though the traveller tell us of the ruins of Egypt, are we so sick or idle, that we must sacrifice our America and today to some man's ill-remembered and indolent story? Carnac and Luxor are but names, or if their skeletons remain, still more desert sand, and at length a wave of the Mediterranean Sea are needed to wash away the filth that attaches to their grandeur. Carnac! Carnac! here is Carnac for me. I behold the columns of a larger and purer temple."

31.5   Hamilcars]   Hamilcar (c. 270–228 BCE) was a Carthaginian statesman and a general in Sicily during the Punic Wars.

34.9   Quonecktacut!]   The Connecticut River.

48.2   The New Colossus]   The sonnet was written in 1883, at the request of an arts group raising money for the construction of a pedestal for the Statue of Liberty, but was not widely known until collected in the author's posthumously published *Poems* (1888). A bronze tablet bearing the text of the sonnet was installed inside the pedestal in 1903.

48.3   brazen giant]   The Colossus of Rhodes, one of the Seven Wonders of the Ancient World.

48.10   twin cities]   New York and Brooklyn.

50.5   hill that Dobell saw]   In "The Common Grave" (1855), one of his many sonnets on the Crimean War, the English poet Sydney Dobell (1824–1874) wrote of war's "great grave upon the hill of blood."

50.7   Burn o' Sorrow . . . Care]   Castle Campbell, in Dollar (or Dolor) Glen, Stirlingshire, Scotland, is a 15th-century structure sited on a hill between two streams, the Burn of Care and the Burn of Sorrow.

Because the Campbells supported Cromwell and his English invaders, Scottish patriots razed most of the castle in 1654.

55.1   *To W. P.*] A sequence of four sonnets dedicated to the memory of Warwick Potter (1870–1893), a young friend of Santayana who died of cholera after a boating accident in France.

61.1   George Crabbe] English poet (1754–1832) who wrote verse-narratives of rural life with a drab uncompromising realism.

64.1   L'Envoi] The final poem in Robinson's collection *The Children of the Night* (1897).

68.1   *Not Always*] A pair of thematically related sonnets in Robinson's collection *Dionysus in Doubt* (1925).

71.6   the edge of doom] Cf. Shakespeare's Sonnet 116, lines 11–12: "Love alters not with his brief hours and weeks, / But bears it out even to the edge of doom."

74.1   Oven Bird] A North American warbler whose dome-shaped nest resembles an oven and whose call sounds like "teacher, teacher."

77.1   The Master Speed] Frost wrote this sonnet as a wedding present for his daughter Irma and John Paine Cone, who were married October 15, 1926.

85.3   Semiramis] Legendary queen of Babylon.

85.4   Skamander] River rising near Mt. Ida and Troy, and flowing into the Hellespont; its Turkish name is Kucuk Menderes.

88.1   *Sonnets from Greece*] A series of five sonnets written April–July 1903 during a tour of Greece, the poet's present to himself upon completing his doctorate in classics at the Sorbonne.

88.2   Helikon] A mountain in Boeotia, in central Greece, from which the fountains of the Muses were said to have sprung.

96.6   Mrs. Grundy's] Mrs. Grundy, a character in Thomas Morton's play *Speed the Plough* (1798), is a stickler for the fine points of propriety; her name has since come to denote the personified force of social convention.

99.2   *And in the Human Heart*] A book-length sequence of 43 Shakespearean sonnets, published in 1940, chronicling the history and vicissitudes of a love affair.

108.1   Gath] One of the five city-states of the Philistines and the birthplace of Goliath.

109.1   *Fatal Interview*] A book-length sequence of 52 sonnets, published in 1931, describing a love affair between the poet in her middle years and a younger man. The title alludes to Donne's Elegy 16, "On His Mistress," which begins: "By our first strange and fatal interview, / By all desires which thereof did ensue . . ."

123.2　　*On Drink*]　The series of three sonnets that opens Putnam's collection *Trinc* (1927).

127.2　　*Mirrors of Venus*]　A book-length sequence of 35 autobiographical sonnets, with the poet's prose commentary, published in 1938.

128.12　　Pathetic Fallacy]　To indulge in the pathetic fallacy is to impute human feelings to non-human entities.

133.15　　Ormus]　Or Hormuz, island in the Strait of Hormuz, the site of an important Arab emporium for the Chinese and Indian trade in the 13th century.

133.15　　Ophir]　Region mentioned in the Old Testament as famous for gold and other expensive commodities.

135.1　　*Sonnets at Christmas*]　A pair of thematically linked sonnets, privately printed in 1934.

136.1　　*More Sonnets at Christmas*]　A series of four sonnets, privately printed in 1942.

136.2　　*Denis Devlin*]　Raised in Dublin, the poet Denis Devlin (1908–1959) was a member of the Irish Diplomatic Service who spent many years in Washington, D.C. There he became a friend of both Allen Tate and Robert Penn Warren, who jointly edited his posthumous *Selected Poems* (1963).

138.2　　Phasellus Ille]　The title alludes to the first line of a poem by Catullus (84–54 BCE): *Phasellus ille quem videtis, hospites, / ait fuisse navium celerrimus* ("The pinnance that you see here, friends, says she was once the fleetest of ships"). Blackmur's sonnet is not a translation but uses Catullus's Latin as its starting point.

139.1　　*Dedications*]　A series of five poems, in a variety of forms, in Blackmur's collection *From Jordan's Delight* (1937).

147.2　　*Berryman's Sonnets*]　A book-length series of 115 sonnets, written in 1947 (as "Sonnets to Chris") and revised, expanded, and published in 1966–67, in which the poet commemorates his spiritual and sexual rebirth through a love affair.

149.5　　Weser]　A river of northwestern Germany that flows through Bremen and enters the North Sea at Bremerhaven.

150.1　　Inauguration Day]　President Dwight D. Eisenhower, affectionately known as "Ike," took the oath of office on January 20, 1953.

150.2　　Stuyvesant]　Stuyvesant Square is a small park on the East Side of Manhattan between 15th Street and 17th Street and First Avenue and Third Avenue. Among its featues is a statue of Peter Stuyvesant (1612–1672), Director-General of the Dutch settlement of New Amsterdam, later New York City.

150.9   Cold Harbor's]   At the battle of Cold Harbor (Hanover, Va., June 3, 1864) the Union suffered 7,000 casualties in one day; General Grant remarked soon after: "I regret this assault more than any one I have ever ordered."

153.2   Miltonic Sonnet]   When this sonnet appeared in *The New York Review of Books* for April 6, 1967, one reader commented that Richard Wilbur, in his title, was confusing "Miltonic" and "Petrarchan." Wilbur replied: "I risked calling my poem 'Miltonic' because it employed the sonnet for a public subject (as in Milton's poems to Vane or Cromwell), because it used Milton's chosen Petrarchan scheme [octave and sestet], and because its one sentence struck me as an unbroken thought."

153.3   Peter Hurd's]   Hurd (1904–1984) was a realist painter known for his depictions of local-color subjects in Texas and the American Southwest. In 1967, President Lyndon B. Johnson commissioned him to paint his official White House portrait but refused the finished work, calling it "the ugliest thing I ever saw." The painting now hangs in the National Portrait Gallery in Washington, D.C.

154.7   the Rospigliosi Cup]   An ornamental cup, of gold, enamel, and pearl, in the collection of the Metropolitan Museum of Art (Fifth Avenue and 82nd Street, New York City). When acquired by the Met in 1912, it was thought to be the work of Benvenuto Cellini (1500–1571); in 1984 it was discovered to be an ingenious fake crafted by the German goldsmith Reinhold Vasters (1827–1909).

158.2   The Poet at Seven]   The title alludes to Rimbaud's poem "Les Poètes de sept ans" (1871), a portrait of the artist as a willful, anarchic, rapacious, and imaginative being.

160.2   Marsyas]   The satyr Marsyas, a master of the flute, challenged Apollo to a musical contest, the loser of which would be at the winner's mercy. When the Muses judged Apollo the better musician, he had Marsyas flayed alive for his presumption.

163.7–8   Al Smith . . . Clemenceau]   Al Smith (1873–1944), two-time governor of New York and Democratic Party candidate for president in 1928; José Maria Sert (1876–1945), Spanish painter and muralist; Georges Clemenceau (1841–1929), French statesman, prime minister during World War I.

INDEX OF POETS, TITLES, AND FIRST LINES

ABOUT THIS SERIES

The American Poets Project offers, for the first time in our history, a compact national library of American poetry. Selected and introduced by distinguished poets and scholars, elegant in design and textually authoritative, the series makes widely available the full scope of our poetic heritage.

For other titles in the American Poets Project, or for information on subscribing to the series, please visit: www.americanpoetsproject.org.

ABOUT THE PUBLISHER

The Library of America, a nonprofit publisher, is dedicated to preserving America's best and most significant writing in handsome, enduring volumes, featuring authoritative texts. For a free catalog, to subscribe to the series, or to learn how you can help support The Library's mission, please visit www.loa.org or write: The Library of America, 14 East 60th Street, New York, NY 10022.

AMERICAN POETS PROJECT

1. **EDNA ST. VINCENT MILLAY** / J. D. McClatchy, editor

2. **POETS OF WORLD WAR II** / Harvey Shapiro, editor

3. **KARL SHAPIRO** / John Updike, editor

4. **WALT WHITMAN** / Harold Bloom, editor

5. **EDGAR ALLAN POE** / Richard Wilbur, editor

6. **YVOR WINTERS** / Thom Gunn, editor

7. **AMERICAN WITS** / John Hollander, editor

8. **KENNETH FEARING** / Robert Polito, editor

9. **MURIEL RUKEYSER** / Adrienne Rich, editor

10. **JOHN GREENLEAF WHITTIER** / Brenda Wineapple, editor

11. **JOHN BERRYMAN** / Kevin Young, editor

12. **AMY LOWELL** / Honor Moore, editor

13. **WILLIAM CARLOS WILLIAMS** / Robert Pinsky, editor

14. **POETS OF THE CIVIL WAR** / J. D. McClatchy, editor

15. **THEODORE ROETHKE** / Edward Hirsch, editor

16. **EMMA LAZARUS** / John Hollander, editor

17. **SAMUEL MENASHE** / Christopher Ricks, editor

18. **EDITH WHARTON** / Louis Auchincloss, editor

19. **GWENDOLYN BROOKS** / Elizabeth Alexander, editor

20. **A. R. AMMONS** / David Lehman, editor

21. **COLE PORTER** / Robert Kimball, editor

22. **LOUIS ZUKOFSKY** / Charles Bernstein, editor

23. **CARL SANDBURG** / Paul Berman, editor

24. **KENNETH KOCH** / Ron Padgett, editor

25. **AMERICAN SONNETS** / David Bromwich, editor